"As nourishing as a three-course Italian feast, this is a fierce, moving tribute to the ties that bind."

—*People* (Book of the Week)

"I loved Lorenzo Carcaterra's *Three Dreamers,* a poignant, unflinching, and uniquely powerful memoir. Carcaterra paints a fascinating, moving, and page-turning portrait of three unforgettable women, each a product of her time, culture, and even location, whether Hell's Kitchen in New York City or the beautiful island of Ischia in Italy. But even more than that, through his transcendent talent, honesty, and emotional intelligence, Carcaterra has created a work that explores what women mean to the men in their lives, writ large. This is a book about love, about family, and about forgiveness. Every mother should read this book."

—LISA SCOTTOLINE,
#1 *New York Times* bestselling author of *Eternal*

"Lorenzo Carcaterra looks back over his life and writes of the women that shaped his worldview. During boyhood summers on Ischia, Lorenzo's Italian grandmother fed him stories and great meals, which built his imagination. His mother, Raffaella, through grief and hardship, sharpened the edges of his ambition, while his wife, Susan, an important journalist, served as the first reader of his bestselling books and a champion of his work. This deeply personal memoir weaves beauty, hilarity, and loss into a glorious tapestry."

—ADRIANA TRIGIANI,
New York Times bestselling author of *Tony's Wife*

"*Three Dreamers* is a stunning triptych—a plaiting together of the lives of three powerful women who, together, have shaped the life and outlook of one man. This beautiful memoir is Lorenzo Carcaterra's tribute to the most important women in his life, and a paean to joy, sorrow, and love."

—ELISSA ALTMAN, author of *Motherland*

"With keen perception and even-keeled acceptance, Carcaterra shares the stories of his grandmother, mother, and wife as he traces how their relationships encouraged him to pursue his dream of becoming a writer."

—*Booklist*

"A moving tribute . . . With spare yet resounding prose, Carcaterra follows these women from his childhood home in Hell's Kitchen to the Italian island of Ischia, to the battles each of them fought at the end of their lives. This emotional narrative isn't for the faint-hearted, but its beauty is a thing to behold."

—*Publishers Weekly* (starred review)

"Engaging . . . This reflective memoir gives nuance to the dark world [Carcaterra] portrays in his novels."

—*Library Journal*

"Elegantly and sensitively written, a book that forges strong connections across four generations."

—*Kirkus Reviews*

THREE

DREAMERS

A Memoir of Family

LORENZO

CARCATERRA

BALLANTINE BOOKS

New York

2022 Ballantine Books Trade Paperback Edition

Copyright © 2021 by Lorenzo Carcaterra

Published in the United States by Ballantine Books, an imprint
of Random House, a division of Penguin Random House LLC, New York.

BALLANTINE and the HOUSE colophon are registered trademarks
of Penguin Random House LLC.

Originally published in hardcover in the United States by
Ballantine Books, an imprint of Random House, a division of
Penguin Random House LLC, in 2021.

Photos courtesy of the author

Library of Congress Cataloging-in-Publication Data

Names: Carcaterra, Lorenzo, author.
Title: Three dreamers / Lorenzo Carcaterra.
Description: First edition. | New York: Ballantine Books, [2021]
Identifier s: LCCN 2020025677 (print) | LCCN 2020025678 (ebook) |
ISBN 9780593156735 | ISBN 9780593156728 (ebook)
Subjects: LCSH: Carcaterra, Lorenzo. | Carcaterra, Lorenzo—Family. |
Carcaterra, Lorenzo—Marriage. | Authors, American—21st century—
Biography. | Italian Americans—Biography. | Women—
Social conditions. | Man-woman relationships.
Classification:L CC PS3553.A653 Z46 2021 (print) | LCC PS3553.A653
(ebook) | DDC 813/.54 [B]—dc23
LC record available at lccn.loc.gov/2020025677
LC ebook record available at lccn.loc.gov/2020025678

Printed in the United States of America on acid-free paper

randomhousebooks.com

1st Printing

Book design by Fritz Metsch

This one is for my daughter, Kate.

She is the next dreamer in the line—
following in the footsteps of Nonna Maria, Grandma Raffaela,
and her mother, Susan. She will do them justice and honor.
They will be proud to have her in their company.
As I am, each and every day.

Men's minds are raised to the level of the women with whom they associate.

—ALEXANDRE DUMAS

CONTENTS

THREE

DREAMERS

INTRODUCTION

I AM SIXTY-SIX years old. I am at a point in life when it is easier to reflect on the past than it is to ruminate on what lies ahead. It is no mystery what awaits me. That inevitable fate lies around a nearby corner, waiting to become a reality, the moment of its arrival known to no one. To say I don't think about the moment would be less than truthful. By the time you reach my age, you have witnessed too much loss, borne the burden of seeing loved ones leave too soon, to not be aware of what lies ahead. But it is much better to not dwell on it and to enjoy what's left of life.

Instead, I choose to spend my time thinking about what brought me here. And, more important, about the people who helped guide me in the direction my life has taken. I think back and see the many faces and hear the many voices that have come into my life through the years. Some were instructive. Some destructive. And some reached out a guiding hand that helped me more than I could ever thank them for.

But the course of my life's voyage, the foundation for the career I have forged, rests in the hands of three very strong-willed and determined women. Each one very different from the other. They helped direct me, each in her own way, toward an honest and productive life.

One, my Nonna Maria, did it through the stories she told, giving me a glimpse into the life she led before me and the losses she bore with dignity, embracing me with a gentle manner and a kindness hidden under a protective shell. She laid down a solid foundation in my younger years, piecing it together across seven glorious summers, confident I would never forget the lessons handed down.

The second, my mother, presented me with a different picture—one of dealing with daily hardship, trapped in a loveless and abusive marriage, cowering under the burden of debt and the stress and fear that came with it. Her words to me, sometimes kind, often bitter, gave fuel to my desire to live as far from such misery as possible. Her lessons were often as harsh as her days, but she passed them on to me with the hope they would drive me from the world we knew to a better one she could only pray I would find.

The third was my wife, an independent woman who was in the process of forging her own career by the time we met. She was smart, pretty, quick to smile, and a gifted editor and writer. She encouraged me to keep writing, despite the obstacles in my path, and out of that a friendship grew. Over time, that friendship led to love and a marriage that lasted for more than three decades, ending with her death from lung cancer on Christmas Eve 2013. We were opposites in many ways—she was the daughter of a doctor and a nurse and grew up in Cincinnati, Ohio. I was the son of an ex-con and a housewife who spoke only Italian and grew up in the Hell's Kitchen neighborhood of Manhattan and the East Bronx. But despite what, on the surface, looked like a storybook childhood, she had undergone her own share of misery and pain. And while there were a few ups and downs in our years together, as there are with any longtime relationships, our love and our friendship never wavered.

Neither did her belief in me and what I could accomplish. Through my bleakest writing years—and there were quite a few—she never let me quit. Giving up was not in her nature—not when she believed in someone as strongly as she believed in me. And when success finally found its way to my door, she was the only one not surprised by its arrival.

These are the three women you are about to meet. I hope you embrace them as I have and take some of their lessons to heart. Trust in their words, take courage from their strength, and gain wisdom from their stories.

They are the women who saved my life.

MARIA

Nonna Maria is seated second from left.

SUMMER 1969

❧

I WAS FOURTEEN when I first set foot on the island of Ischia, eighteen miles off the coast of Naples, Italy.

I was visiting my mother's side of the family, strangers to me in every way, and I had no idea what to expect. Yet, somehow, as soon as I stepped off the boat from Naples, surrounded by thick hordes of tourists and locals eager to get to their destination, I knew I was in a better place than the one I had left behind.

I arrived in Ischia a troubled teenager. Back in New York, I left parents waging a daily war over heavy debts and mounting bills, their anger always at full boil, my mother one stinging comment away from receiving a fatal blow at my father's hand. The constant squabbles, the scams and cons my father pulled on gullible friends and neighbors, hung heavy on my shoulders, with my own fears and concerns. I wanted a different life from the dead-end existence that engulfed me in New York, but I couldn't figure out where that life would be or where it would lead.

I had argued without success against coming to Ischia, preferring to join friends and a cousin for a month of baseball camp. But money for baseball camp was scarce, especially when a round-trip coach ticket on Alitalia cost a mere sixty-eight dollars, and my father's fear of the drugs that had invaded our neighborhood far outweighed any qualms I had about getting on a plane to Rome, a train to Naples, and a boat to Ischia.

At least I knew there would be no language barrier to overcome.

My mother never bothered to learn English, and the only language I spoke until I started grade school was Italian, specifically the Southern Italian dialect spoken on Ischia. And I had been raised on a steady diet of pasta with clam sauce on Fridays, pasta with red sauce on Sundays, and pasta with lentils or beans or squid or oil and garlic the rest of the week, so I didn't imagine food would be an issue.

I picked up my bags and made my way through the port, passing massive buses filled with German tourists and cabs waiting to take passengers to their hotels. I spotted several horse-drawn carriages parked on side streets and walked past a handful of coffee bars and gelato stands. In every corner of the port, men stood in small circles, smoking and waving their hands, engaged in animated discussions; old women walked slowly under a hot morning sun, arms linked together in a casual embrace, many wearing loose-fitting summer dresses; younger women, most of them pushing small children in snug strollers, made their way through the crowd, bathing suits clearly visible under their thin wraparounds. It was all so different from the world I had left behind. The sounds, smells, sights were all foreign, but somehow I knew from those very first moments it was a world where I truly belonged.

I reached into the front pocket of my jeans and pulled out a folded piece of paper. My mother had written out the simple set of directions I would need to reach my grandmother's home.

I walked up Via Roma and made a sharp left just before the start of the steep hill that led to Saint Peter's Church. A quarter of the way into the narrow walkway, I turned right and took two steps down into a small square that had a stone wall on one side and three homes on the other. It was here, at the last house in the square, that I first saw my Italian grandmother, Maria Mattera Carcaterra.

She was wearing a widow's black blouse, long skirt, and black sandals. Her thick hair, rolled in the back into a circular bun, was as white as a cloud. She waited until I was at the base of the stairway and casually waved me up. She then turned and headed back into her home, walking with a slight limp favoring her right leg. I made it up the stairs and rested my bags in the foyer. The walls were made of stone and painted white, the large room dominated by a dining table and two small couches. There were two large framed photos on opposite walls, each encased in a thick old wooden frame. One I knew must be of my grandfather, Gabriel, clearly taken when he was a young man. Nonna Maria came out of the kitchen and looked at me. Her eyes were dark and penetrating but with a hint of mischief in them. She stepped closer to me and I reached out my right hand, ready to shake hers and kiss her on both cheeks, as I had been told was the customary way to greet friends and family. She ignored my outstretched hand and wrapped her arms around me, holding me close to her for several moments, neither one of us saying a word. She then kissed me on top of my head, held me for a few seconds longer, and relaxed her arms. "The bathroom is down the hall," she said in Italian, nodding toward the rear of the apartment as she made her way back to the kitchen. "Wash up, change clothes if you like. Take any of the back rooms. Lunch will be ready in about ten minutes. You should be hungry after such a long trip."

I picked up my bags and looked into the kitchen as I made my way toward the hallway off the living room. "My mom told me you're a great cook," I said.

She turned toward me, a large wooden spoon in her right hand, pots and pans taking up every inch of the stove top. Behind her were an assortment of plates filled with roasted peppers, marinated eggplant, grilled artichokes, and a tomato and red onion salad. Nonna looked at me and shrugged. "I don't do anything," she said. "The stove does all the work."

By the time I came back into the main room of the house, the dining table was filled with platters of food. I sat on a hardback wood chair and waited for Nonna to come join me. She walked in holding a pot of espresso in one hand and a small cup in the other and sat across from me, the framed photo of my grandfather, her husband, gazing down at her. She nodded to the bottle of wine in the center of the table. "Eat and drink as much as you want," she said. "There's plenty more of everything in the kitchen. Your mother lets you have wine with your meals?"

I nodded. "Since I was four years old," I said. "She mixes it with water."

"Water is for flowers," Nonna said, reaching for the bottle of red wine and pouring me half a glass.

Her arms were folded on the table, one gnarled hand on top of the other, the coffee cup resting between them. "Aren't you going to eat?" I asked.

She gazed down at her cup of coffee. "This is all I need for now," she said.

I filled my plate and ate in silence for several minutes while Nonna refilled her coffee cup. "Is this where I'll be staying?" I finally asked, as I cut through a large stuffed red pepper. "Here with you?"

"My door is always open," Nonna said. "You can stay here for the summer or spend some time in the apartment building on Via Casciaro. Many of your aunts, uncles, and cousins are spending the summer there. It would be good for you to get to know them. For you to meet your family. But that's up to you."

"Do you go there a lot?" I asked.

"I've never been there," Nonna said. "I don't think I ever will go. I had it built for my children and for their children. I belong here, in my own home."

"It must be nice," I said. "To have your own home, I mean. We don't have anything like this in New York. The apartment we just moved into is about as big as this room."

Nonna sipped her coffee and nodded. "You have your own home. Here, in Ischia."

"I don't know what you mean."

"The building on Via Casciaro has twelve apartments," Nonna said. "They were divided equally between my six children; each got two apartments. They drew straws as to who would get which. Your mother got one of the garden apartments and one on the top floor. You're the youngest of her sons, so you get the one-bedroom. The one in the garden. It's yours. Not today, but one day."

"I bet it's better than what we're living in back home," I said. "That was a nice thing for you to do. Not for me, I mean. For your family."

"You are my family," Nonna said.

She stood slowly and began to clear the table. I got up to help her, and she looked at me and shook her head. "I'll take care of this," she said. "Go in the back and get some rest. Later, when you wake up from your nap, you'll go and meet the rest of your family. They're all waiting to see you, especially the cousins your age."

"How many cousins my age do I have?" I asked.

"On this island," Nonna said, as she headed back into the kitchen, "more than you can count."

OVER THE NEXT two weeks, I met my aunts, uncles, and cousins and made a number of friends. As with my initial feelings about the island, there was an immediate sense of comfort and ease as I got to know the members of my mother's family. From the very first moment we met, we bonded as if I had been coming there every summer my whole life. I grew close to my cousin Paolo, and he introduced me to two of his friends—Pepe and Gaspare. We were all around the same age and the four of us soon became inseparable. We went to the beach in the mornings, swimming the hours away in the cool if crowded waters. Our nights were spent exploring the port, occasionally stopping for a simple pizza dinner, followed by a late-night walk and a gelato.

My uncles owned a tour company, and we would ride for free on the big buses with the family name written across the sides. I toured the eighteen-square-mile island several times, always struck by its beauty. The tourists were mostly German or British, many of whom had been coming to Ischia for years. My Uncle Mario spoke fluent German, and there were a number of tour guides fluent in multiple languages. During those two-hour rides around the island, I took in as much of its history as I could absorb—from its volcanic inception to its famed mineral waters and thermal baths to its occupation by the Nazis during World War II.

It was, by far, the happiest period of my life. It was so easy, at least for a brief time, to forget the horrors of what I had left behind in New York. My aunts—my mom's sisters, Nancy, Anna, and Frances—treated me as if I were one of their sons. Their husbands were equally warm and eager to make sure I felt welcome. My young cousins and their friends were fun to be around and made the time spent in their company memorable.

Each day, whether early in the morning or around sunset, I made it a point to visit with Nonna. She always had the coffeepot percolating regardless of time of day, and I loved sitting with her—either in her living room or after the short walk up the hill to Saint Peter's Church. She liked to sit on the stone bench in front of the church, in the cool of the night, watching as the tourists walked Corso Vittoria Colonna, dressed in their finest summer clothes.

In the short time I had spent in her company, I had already come to know several things about Nonna. She was a private person and never asked anyone a personal question, no matter how innocent it might appear. By the same token, she never wanted to be asked anything personal.

One night, after dinner, the two of us were sitting on the stone bench, quietly watching the crowd make their way past the shops, restaurants, and bars that dotted the Corso. A middle-aged man in a crisp polo shirt, creased shorts, and sandals walked by and nodded to Nonna.

"Buona sera, Maria," he said, waving and coming closer to us.

Nonna nodded and gave him a short wave.

"Is this your grandson?" he asked, pointing at me as he approached. "The one from America?"

Nonna nodded again. "Yes," she said. "This is him."

"Bravo," he said with a wide smile. "And what great meal did you prepare for your grandson tonight? I only wish I was there, knowing what a great cook you must be."

Nonna smiled. "We both had steak, string beans with oil, lemon, and garlic, and a nice tomato salad."

The man smiled and clasped his hands together. "Excellent, Maria," he said. "Keep it up and the boy will never want to go back to America."

With that he wished us a good night, waved, and continued his walk down the Corso.

When he was safely out of earshot, I looked at her. "Nonna, we had pasta with clam sauce for dinner," I said to her. "We didn't have steak."

Nonna turned to me and shrugged. "Why is it any of his business what we had for dinner?" she said. "We ate what we ate. That should only matter to you and to me."

It was not Nonna's way to lecture or admonish. She never raised her voice and was most at home in the company of her grown children and a platoon of grandchildren in all age groups. She allowed the younger ones to rummage through the flowered apron she wore around her waist when she was in her kitchen, gleefully helping themselves to the wide array of candies she kept stashed in the two front pockets. She laughed and caressed their faces as each grandchild came away with fists full of hard candy. And if one of her daughters complained that the children should be limited to one or two sweets, Nonna would shrug her shoulders. "I didn't give them anything," she would say. "They took what they wanted." The sentence was always followed by a wink and a nod at the closest grandchild.

Nonna's family was from Ischia Ponte, a neighborhood that abuts the port. Its main attraction is the famous Castello Aragonese, used centuries ago as a defense against invaders. Today it is a tourist destination, complete with a small hotel and Il Monastero, a restaurant that offers a top-tier menu and magnificent views of the bay.

Ischia Ponte is a poorer area than the port or any of the other five boroughs that make up the island of Ischia. It is home to the many fishermen of the area, and these days the backstreets leading to the castle are crammed with small houses, bunched tightly together. On hot summer nights, old men and women sit on garden chairs in front of their homes; young children squat in the sand a few feet away, small pail and scoop at the ready; teens play soccer games closer to the beach, using large plastic garbage cans as makeshift goals. All in an attempt to catch a breeze and pass another scorching night. Ischia Ponte is crowded in the summer months and desolate in the winter.

During tourist season, street musicians gather in front of a small square or on the mile-long stone walkway to the castle entrance and serenade evening strollers, straw baskets or hats resting in front of them, which they hope to see filled with euros before the night comes to an end.

The highlight of the season arrives on July 26, the feast of Saint Anne. On this night, the bay is packed with tourist and fishing boats, all lit with torches, and wood and straw laid outside the castle is set ablaze. Larger boats come flowing down from the port, a convoy of multicolored floats, one of which will be designated best in show before the evening's end. And then a large and expansive series of fireworks is set off.

When she was a girl, Nonna would stand by the water's edge and watch the display with awe and fascination. By the time I met her, she had not been to the feast since my grandfather Gabriel died in 1954. "I remember all the times I went to see it," she said to me. "From when I was a child to when I was married with children of my own. I don't need to see it again. I just remember the times I went. As you get older, the memory of a place is better than being there. At least it is for me."

Nonna met Gabriel while she was still a teenager and, by all accounts, it was love at first glance. Gabriel was a shepherd from the port area, with enough family land to support a small flock. They were married in the early years of the twentieth century and shortly after moved into the home where Nonna would live until the day she died. They adored one another, seldom argued, and together raised a family and opened a successful fruit-and-vegetable business. Gabriel had a golden heart, lending what money and clothing he could spare to those in greater need. That became harder to do in the years leading up to World War II. When war finally did arrive, it made daily living that much more difficult. Survival became the family's only goal.

Nonna and Nonno, then both in their forties, suffered through great loss during those dark years, as did everyone on the island. But they soldiered on, moving forward, looking to ensure that their family of seven children had clothes to wear and food to eat.

During those turbulent times, Nonna would leave her house under the shade of early-morning darkness and make the trip to Naples in search of black-market goods. In the decades before hydrofoils, the ninety-minute trek by boat to Naples from the island seemed to last as long as an ocean crossing, and the big old ships—often working off rationed gas and in constant need of repair—would sometimes stall on the open sea, floating aimlessly for hours on end until a crew member could remedy the problem.

Once in Naples, Nonna would walk the bombed and ruined streets in search of bread, olive oil, coffee, milk, and, on rare occasions, red meat or chicken. She would pay the black marketers in lira and bundle up whatever she was able to purchase in a pouch hidden under her dress. Then, as quickly as she could, she would make her way back to the port for the return trip to Ischia.

It was dangerous and draining work, made more so when both the island and the city of Naples were under Nazi occupation. The Nazis imposed a 10 P.M. curfew, and most of the islanders obeyed the order rather than risk the wrath of the soldiers patrolling the streets and alleys.

But not Nonna.

Two nights a week, Nonna and two others—both men, and longtime family friends—would meet at the highest point of the island, in the borough of Serrara Fontana, where the large vineyard was located. One of the men sat on top of a wooden cart pulled by a mule. Inside the cart were three oak barrels filled with white wine. The wheels of the cart and the hooves of the mules were wrapped in thick rags, to help silence any noise as they began their descent down the slippery stone steps toward the port. It would take them four hours to complete their task, starting at midnight and reaching the harbor before sunup. There, they would be greeted by two men from Naples in a rowboat. The barrels would be transferred from the cart to the rowboat. Once the task was completed, one of the men in the boat would hand over a small wad of lira to Nonna, and then the two would row as slowly and quietly as possible away from the edge of the pier to a motorboat moored three miles offshore. The money Nonna earned was used to purchase black-market clothes for her children and family members in need.

I first heard about Nonna helping to move shipments of black-market wine from Angela Rumore, one of the friends I made during those early weeks on the island. "My grandmother used to tell me the story when I was younger," she said to me as we both walked along the Lido, a long stretch of promenade that faced the sea, the lights from the surrounding islands glistening under the warm blanket of a summer night. "The walk was slow and dangerous. There were Nazis everywhere, and anyone who broke curfew risked getting shot. It was hard work, keeping the cart from making noise, making sure the mule didn't slip on the rocks and grass. It was all downhill, and your Nonna and the others had to walk in bare feet. That made it even scarier. To this day, she never talks about it. The other two did—that's where my mother first heard it, from one of them. But not a word about those nights from your grandmother."

"Why do you think that is?" I asked.

Angela shrugged. She was a year older than me, her brown hair long and streaked blond by the sun, her smile open and warm. "Maybe there are some things she would rather not remember or have to think about," she said. "Some things from that war she would like to forget."

"She could have been killed," I said. "If any of the soldiers saw or heard them. They might have taken them prisoner or, worse, shot and killed them right there on the spot."

"My mother told me it was so bad here during the war and the years after," Angela said, stopping to look out at the lapping waves below. "They were afraid to drink the water because it had been polluted from the bombings and smelled when it came out of the faucets. There was no work for anyone, little food, and no help from Rome or anywhere else. She told me the lucky ones were the ones who died, not the ones who had to live through those years."

I WAS EAGER to hear more about Nonna's exploits during the war years. I knew I would never hear the stories from Nonna herself, so Angela became my primary source. I was at Angela's apartment one afternoon, sitting in her living room, both of us drinking English breakfast tea.

"Your grandmother has really made an impression on you," she said.

"I've never met anyone like her," I said. "I could sit in her dining room and listen to her stories all day. She's a born storyteller. And I bet she's never read a book or a magazine or a newspaper in her life."

"Your Nonna has lived a life that's more interesting than any book you'll read or any story you can find in a paper or a magazine," Angela said. "She's much tougher than she looks and has the courage of a lion. She won't say that about herself. But ask anyone who's heard the stories about her, especially during those war years, and they'll tell you."

"How come you know so many of them?"

"Your Nonna and my grandparents are close friends, have been since they were young," she said. "So, what I heard about your Nonna, I heard from them, when I was a little girl."

"My Aunt Frances told me she was almost killed," I said. "During a bombing raid in Naples."

"More than once," Angela said. "She was fearless. I guess she had no choice. There was one time, she and my grandfather got off the boat from Naples. It was just about sunup, the streets still damp and dark. They started walking to their homes, using side streets and shadows to avoid being seen by the Nazi soldiers on patrol."

"They must have come back from Naples with something for them to be that careful," I said.

"They *always* came back from Naples with something," Angela said. "Especially your Nonna. She never left empty-handed. On this day, she had two round loaves of bread and a large chunk of cheese hidden in a cloth under her dress. It was enough to feed the family for a day, maybe even two."

"Did she get stopped?" I asked.

Angela nodded. "A few streets from her house. My grandfather was about four buildings ahead of her. They thought it was safer to walk separately; this way only one of them would get caught if they were spotted by the Nazis."

"So, what happened?"

"A Nazi soldier turned a corner and he almost bumped into Nonna," Angela said. "They stared at each other for a few seconds. Then the soldier took a few steps back and aimed his rifle at her. My grandfather, hiding in the shadows, pulled a knife from his pouch and started moving closer to them."

Angela stood and walked out of the living room. "Where are you going?" I asked. "You can't leave in the middle of a story."

"Relax, American," she said. "I'll be back in a second. I'm just getting us some water."

She came back into the room holding a bottle of mineral water and two glasses. She sat down, filled both glasses, and took a long drink from one. "The Nazis had been here long enough to have learned a few Italian words," she said, resting her glass on the coffee table. "And my grandfather and your Nonna knew a few phrases in German."

"It couldn't have been more than 'thank you' and 'please don't shoot,' " I said.

"The soldier lifted the front of his rifle up and down and asked Nonna to raise her hands," Angela said. "Now, if she did as he asked, the bread and the cheese she had wrapped under her blouse would fall to the ground. She couldn't let that happen."

"What did she do?"

"She stepped up closer to the soldier," Angela said. "He was young, not more than a boy, really. Nonna looked into his eyes and told him she had a son his age and that he had died in the war. Then she told him she had bread and cheese she brought from Naples and needed to bring that food to her family. They were hungry and were waiting to eat. So, she was going to walk past him and go home. That was what she had to do. He was a soldier and he had a rifle and she would understand if he did what he needed to do."

"Did he understand anything she said?" I asked.

"He must have understood something," Angela said. "He held his rifle on her for a moment and then watched as Nonna turned her back and began to walk away from him. My grandfather was still watching from the shadows as your Nonna walked past him. He looked over at the soldier. He had slowly lowered his rifle and watched her disappear down a side street."

I leaned my head back and stared up at the white ceiling. Angela finished the last of her water. We sat in silence for several moments. "We will never know the kind of courage it takes to do something like that," Angela said.

"No," I said, shaking my head. "Not even close."

I WAS SITTING at Nonna's dining room table, in my now-usual spot across from her, looking up at a framed photo of a handsome young man who seemed to be only a few years older than me. The frame was made of thick wood and must have weighed close to ten pounds, with curved edges carved in four corners. But as imposing as the frame looked—matching the one behind me that held my grandfather's photo—it merely highlighted the face of the man staring back at me. His hair was black, curled and thick, and his eyes were the color of coal. He wasn't smiling, but his face had a warm glow.

I looked away from the photo as Nonna came into the room. She was holding a tray with two cups of coffee, the ever-present pot of espresso, a sugar bowl, and a plate filled with assorted pastries. She rested the tray on the table and poured out two cups of coffee. She passed the sugar and one of the cups to me and then sat down. "They're still hot," she said, nodding toward the pastries. "The girl from Minicucci's delivered them just before you got here. Have as many as you want."

I held the hot cup of coffee and looked up at the photo of the young man. I had been wanting to ask Nonna about him since my first night in her home but thought it best to wait until we had grown comfortable with each other.

"Nonna, who is that?" I asked, my eyes still on the photo.

She didn't bother turning around. Nonna poured two large scoops of sugar in her coffee and stirred it, her eyes on the dark liquid. "That's your Uncle John," she said.

By this time, after nearly three weeks on the island, I thought I had met all my aunts and uncles. I took a sip of hot coffee and looked from the photo back to Nonna. "I haven't met him yet," I said. "He's not here, in Ischia?"

Nonna sat back in her chair, her hands resting on top of the table. She looked at me for a few moments. "I was in Naples, at the hospital," she said in a soft voice. "I had just given birth to my last child, your Uncle Joseph."

"I've met him," I said. "He lets me ride on his bus if there's an extra seat. I've toured the island with him a couple of times."

Nonna nodded, a slight smile on her wrinkled face. "The day came for us to go home—me, my husband, and the new baby. While I was getting dressed, the nuns were out in the big room preparing the babies to leave. Your grandfather stood off to the side, watching as they changed and dressed the babies. He was leaning against a wall and noticed there was a baby in a crib in a far corner, away from the others. The nuns weren't getting him ready."

"Why not?"

"That's what your grandfather wanted to know," Nonna said. "He went over to the Mother Superior. They knew each other well—we had been to the hospital many times over the years. She looked at my husband and then at the baby. The Mother Superior shook her head and told him that the baby had been abandoned. He was no one's child."

"Abandoned?" I said. "You mean left on their front door, like that?"

"I'm not sure where he was left," Nonna said, "but there were no parents around to take him home. Your grandfather stayed quiet for a few moments, his eyes on the abandoned baby. Then he looked back at the Mother Superior and asked, 'What will happen to him?' "

Nonna finished her cup of coffee, then reached for the still-warm espresso pot and poured herself another. "The Mother Superior told your grandfather that once all the other babies left with their families, they would prepare the baby, a boy, and take him to the orphanage a few miles from the hospital. He would be cared for there and raised along with the other orphans. Your grandfather looked at the Mother Superior and then back at the baby boy in the corner. He stayed quiet for a while and then asked her, 'Can I take him home with us?' "

Nonna paused to pour two large scoops of sugar into her coffee and stirred them in slowly. She closed her eyes for a moment and wiped at her forehead with a cloth napkin in her left hand. "Mother Superior thought about it for a minute or two and then nodded. She told your grandfather he would need to sign some papers back in her office. Once that was done, then, yes, he would be allowed to take the baby home and raise him as his own."

"He never came to talk to you about it?" I asked. "Before he went and signed the papers?"

Nonna shook her head and smiled. "It wouldn't have changed anything if he had," she said. "But, no, he didn't ask me. The first time I saw the baby, I was putting on my coat to leave the hospital. Two nuns wheeled in two cribs, your grandfather standing behind them, a wide smile on his face. I looked at the two babies and then at him. 'I'll tell you all about it on the boat back to Ischia' is all he said to me."

Nonna leaned back in her chair. It was a warm day, and a thin line of sweat had formed on her upper lip. "We named the baby John. Now, you know, no parent will admit to having a favorite among their children. But John and your grandfather had a connection from the very first day. When John got older, he would go out in the fields with my husband to help him tend to the flock. He was good with his hands, and he helped your grandfather build shelves and a toolshed and even that extra room downstairs. They were as close as any father and son."

I nodded and looked up at the framed photo of the uncle I was hearing about for the first time. Nonna took a slow, deep breath and continued. "Then came a war none of us asked for and John went off to fight," she said. "He joined the Navy and was put on submarine duty. One night, an English warship sent down bombs that explode underwater. I forget now what they call them."

"Depth charges," I said. "There's a show on American TV I watch with my father sometimes, *Victory at Sea.* That's what they call them."

"They sent down enough of them that it destroyed the submarine and killed everyone inside," Nonna said. "My boy died such a horrible death. I can't imagine the pain and fear he must have felt. A few months later, a big car pulled up on the road just beyond the house. Your grandfather happened to be home that day, working on one of the outside walls, standing halfway up a ladder. He turned when he saw the car. A priest was the first one out, then a soldier with a lot of medals on his chest. He was holding a wooden box with a flag on top. They were about to come toward the house. Your grandfather held up a hand and told them not to move. 'Do you have my son?' he asked them. 'If you don't have my son, then get back in your car and leave.'

"The priest tried to calm him down. 'Gabriel,' he said, 'they are here to offer their sympathy and give you some of your son's personal effects.' Your grandfather glared at them and said, 'The only thing I want is my son. Not their sympathy, not their flag, not their medals. Just my boy.' "

Nonna stared at the table for several minutes, her hands curled around the cloth napkin, her voice filled with a sadness the weight of which I could never imagine. "Cancer took your grandfather's life eleven years later," she said after several long moments of silence. "But to me, he died on that day, standing on that ladder, knowing that John was dead."

She pushed back her chair, stood, and glanced up at the framed photo of the young man with the handsome face. "That's who is in that picture," she said. "My son. Your uncle. His name is John, and he was nineteen years old when he died."

She walked back into her kitchen and stood against the sink, running the cold water and staring out the window.

IT HAD BEEN easy for me to grow close to my cousins and the friends they introduced me to during my early weeks in Ischia. They were—boys and girls alike—open and welcoming and I felt comfortable in their company. I had a few close friends back in New York, but we were all from the same neighborhood, and their home lives were similar to my own. With the shadow of what awaited us when we returned to our apartments lurking over us at all times, it was hard to be as free and relaxed as I was on the island.

One early evening I was walking next to my cousin Paolo, our friends Gaspare and Pepe next to us. Gaspare was Ischia born and bred and was seldom without a smile on his face. Pepe lived with his family in Rome and spent his summers on Ischia, living with his grandmother. He was the most serious of the group and was curious about my life back in America. "Do you know how to shoot pool?" he asked me. "Do you have that game in New York?"

I had never shot a game of pool in my life. What little I knew about it came from watching the Paul Newman movie *The Hustler* with my father, reading a book about Minnesota Fats, and seeing the great Willie Mosconi shoot a few games on television. But I was not going to let my Ischia pals in on my lack of skills. "I can shoot," I said. "You have pool halls here?"

"There's one a little farther up the street," Gaspare said. "It should be open by now."

"What's your game?" Pepe asked.

"Nine ball," I said, using up the only pool terminology I knew.

"Do you play for money in New York or for fun?" Paolo asked.

"Both," I said. "But let's just play for fun. I'd feel bad taking all your money."

"In your dreams, American," Pepe said, smiling. "If money is going to change hands, it's going to end up in my pocket, not yours."

The pool hall was large and empty. There were a few chairs scattered about and a small table in a corner, where four old men were in the middle of a card game. There was a bar that served coffee, mineral water, and soda. Paolo went up to the middle-aged man behind the bar and asked how much it would cost to shoot a few rounds of pool. The man turned and glanced at the large clock above his head. "It's quiet now," he said. "And it's still early. The table's yours until the regulars start to come in. Don't make too much noise, buy a few bottles of water, and have a good time."

Gaspare racked the balls, and I went over and selected a pool cue from the wide assortment lined up against a far wall. "You break, American," he said to me, once the pool balls were in place.

I remembered enough from the movie to know you broke and shot with the white ball. I placed the ball on its mark and then spent several minutes studying the table, or pretending to study the table. I placed the far end of the pool cue between my thumb and index finger, as I had seen the great Mosconi do on television. I took a deep breath and put the cue to the ball.

I watched as the ball sailed off the table and nearly hit Paolo in the face before landing on the wood floor next to his feet. "It's pool, cousin," he said to me. "Not soccer."

Pepe shook his head and Gaspare laughed. "Maybe you play it a different way in America," Gaspare said. "Maybe you keep score by how many times you hit people in the head instead of how many balls you put into the pockets."

I rested my pool cue against the table and shrugged. "That was the first time I've ever hit a pool ball," I said. "I just didn't want you guys to think I was a loser."

Pepe put an arm around my shoulders. "We would never think that about you," he said. "And you shouldn't think it about us. We don't need to impress each other. We're friends. That's all that matters."

"But since we now know you can't play at all," Gaspare said, "maybe we should play a few games for money."

Paolo grabbed a pool cue and stepped up in front of the table, stick in his hand. "I'll break," he said. "Watch where I place the stick between my fingers. And you don't want to hit the ball either too hard or too soft."

I watched as the ball hit the middle of the rack and sent the packed balls heading off in all directions across the table, two of them landing in corner pockets. "You see," Paolo said, nodding at me. "It's as easy as kissing a girl on the lips."

I looked at Paolo and took the cue from his hand. "I've never kissed a girl on the lips," I said.

"One thing at a time," Pepe said. "Let's teach you how to shoot a game of pool first. Then we'll worry about how to kiss a girl."

"Lucky for you, we have all summer," Paolo said. "And besides, if you can't find a girl to kiss on this island, then you won't find a girl anywhere."

"Not even in New York?" I said, smiling along with them.

"New York may be an island," Gaspare said. "But we're the island of love. You're in the right place."

MY HAPPY TIMES on the island were still not enough to set me free from the haunting memories of the life I had left behind in New York. In my quiet moments I flashed on my parents, alone now, their daily lives filled with brutality, infidelity, and debt. I could never lose that sense of dread that comes with not knowing at what hour of the day or night the shouts and screams will start, a volley of dishes thrown against walls, the sound of a folded belt snapping against soft flesh. You spend years living with those horrendous sounds, they are forever seared into the darkest recesses of your brain. You can never forget them and you never will, no matter where your life takes you.

But at least for those first three weeks in Ischia, during my first summer away from home, those sounds briefly faded from my mind. My cousins and new friends helped. My aunts and uncles helped even more. But no one helped silence those sounds more than my Nonna.

I was sitting with Nonna on the stone bench in front of Saint Peter's. It was early evening, and the warmth of late June had turned into the blistering heat of mid-July, the humidity in the air strong enough to touch. Nonna sat to my right, cooling herself with a black hand fan, her eyes on the endless parade of locals and tourists passing by. "I spoke to your mother today," she said. "She'll be here early next month."

I nodded. "Only for about ten days," I said. "She can't leave my father alone for too long."

Nonna closed up her fan and rested it between us. "She asked me how you were doing here," she said.

"What did you tell her?"

"To ask you," Nonna said. "Good time or bad, you should be the one to tell her, not me."

"I'm having a great time, Nonna," I said. "I wish I didn't have to go home next month."

Nonna rested a hand on my arm and smiled. "Your mother told me you want to be a writer," she said. "What does a writer do?"

"Tell stories," I said. "I don't even know why I told her that."

"Stories," Nonna said. "Like the ones in those books you're reading all the time?"

"The stories in those books are great ones," I said. "I don't have great stories to tell."

Nonna turned back to look at the passing crowd. "Life will give you all the great stories you need," she said.

An elderly couple walked arm in arm past us and waved and smiled at Nonna. She was quick to return the wave and the smile.

"That's Patrizia's mother and father," Nonna said. "I see she is among the group of friends you and Paolo spend time with."

I nodded. "She's very nice," I said. "I met her sisters the other day. They're both much older than she is."

Nonna stood and waited for me to do the same. She placed her left hand under the crook of my right arm, and we started our slow walk back to her house. "During the war, Patrizia's father went into the army," Nonna said, walking with her head down, the limp in her right leg more pronounced as we moved down the sloping street. "He left behind a wife and those two sisters you met the other day. They were both very young then. At first he sent letters to his wife, along with some money. After a few months the letters stopped arriving. A year went by with no word. Then, one day, his wife got a letter from the army. They wrote to tell her that her husband was missing in action and thought to be dead. Those years were desperate times for many on this island. Especially for a young woman with two small children to feed."

"What did she do?"

"What she needed to do to feed her children," Nonna said. "The island was occupied by the Nazis in those years and she spent time with some of the soldiers, earning money that bought what food she could get on the black market."

I looked over at Nonna. She was still walking with her head

down, focused on every small step she was taking, her words and her thoughts in a past that could never be forgotten. "A few years after that, the war ended and the soldiers left," she said. "Then, six months later, her husband, the man everyone thought was dead, gets off a boat from Naples. Turns out he had been in a prison camp in North Africa. Now, you've been here long enough to know her husband wasn't back for more than fifteen minutes before a dozen people told him what his wife had done in the years he was gone. He was, as you can expect, angry, embarrassed, not sure what to do. One minute he wanted to kill her, the next minute he wanted to kill himself. Those early days back were hard ones for him and for his wife."

"So what did he end up doing?" I asked.

"He went to see a priest and your grandfather," Nonna said. "He needed time to think it all out and calm himself down so he wouldn't do something he would come to regret."

"What did they tell him?"

"Your grandfather did most of the talking," Nonna said. "He took him up to the fields, watching over what was left of the flock. They had some wine and cheese together. Your grandfather pointed out that the husband was still a young man, plenty of time for him to meet another woman, maybe even fall in love with her. Make a life with this new woman."

"Nonno thought he should leave his wife?" I asked.

"He was just showing the man one of the roads he could go down," Nonna said. "But then both your grandfather and the priest asked the husband to think of two things before he decided. The first was, how would he know what this new woman did during the war to survive? It could have been the very same thing his wife had done. But, they both pointed out to the husband, they knew for certain what this new woman had not done during the time he was away."

"What?"

"She didn't keep his children fed and alive," Nonna said. "His wife had. Then they left him with a decision to make, one that proved easy once he took the time to think it over."

"So, he went back to his wife?"

Nonna nodded. "It wasn't easy at first," she said. "They slept in separate rooms of the house for a few years and barely spoke to one another. But, with time, they grew closer together and they started to once again share the same bed. They became what they were always meant to be—a husband and wife in love with each other. Soon after that, Patrizia was born. And look at them now, walking arm in arm, as happy as when they were young, in the years before the war ripped them apart."

"I'm glad they stayed together," I said.

We had reached Nonna's house, and she stopped at the base of the stairs to catch her breath. "Let me ask you," she said, "did you like that story I just told?"

"Yes," I said. "I liked it a lot."

"Was it as good as some of the stories you read in your books?"

"Yes," I said, smiling. "It was."

She rested a hand on top of mine. "If that's true, then I could be a writer, no?"

"Yes, Nonna," I said, holding the smile. "You could be a writer, too."

"And if I can be a writer," she said, "then you can be, too. That story belongs to you now. It's free for you to tell."

Nonna let go of my hand, grasped the railing leading up to the second floor of her home, and began the slow walk up the thick stone steps.

I watched her go up, knowing she would refuse my help. I stayed at the base of the stairwell for several moments, tears running down the sides of my face. The strength and clarity of her story affected me deeply. But more than that, the passing of the story on to me was the most beautiful and precious gift anyone had ever given me. A gift I would never forget.

MY HAPPY SUMMER on Ischia came to a sudden halt the morning after my mother, Raffaela, arrived on the island. I met her on the crowded beach a short distance from Nonna's house. She was standing with her back to me, water lapping onto her feet, the morning sun warming her face. I stood next to her and we both stayed quiet for several moments, taking in the sounds of the children playing around us and the older kids kicking a soccer ball into the water and then diving in after it. "I need to tell you something," my mother said. "About your father. About something he did. Something you need to know."

I closed my eyes and shook my head. "How much does he owe this time?" I asked.

"It's not about money," my mother said.

I turned to look at her and caught the sadness etched across my mother's face. I saw how much it diminished her and made her look much older than her years.

"What, then?"

"It's about his first wife," my mother said. "And the way she died."

My parents were both previously married. And they were both somewhat secretive about their past spouses, my father more so. I knew my mother's first husband was a carabiniere, a federal officer from Northern Italy, and that together they had two children, both sons. One of her boys—a six-month-old infant—died during World War II, as did her husband. What they died of was never made clear to me. My mother often blamed the war and occasionally would mention an illness, but she was never specific. She was widowed for eight years before she agreed to marry my father.

I had also been told that my father was previously married and that his first wife died of an illness, most likely cancer. I was never supposed to talk to him about her, since her death brought up so many horrible memories for him. I did notice that on the rare occasions when her death was mentioned, the cause often changed. One time it was an illness, another time a car accident, a third time she had a stroke. I was either too young or too naïve to question the discrepancies.

"What about the way she died?" I asked.

"She didn't die of cancer," my mother said. "That's what he wants you to believe. He murdered her."

She spoke without fear or apprehension, just sadness. She was home, on her island, surrounded by her family and away from my father, finally free to speak the truth. "He strangled her with a pillow in a hotel room. And he went to prison for it."

I stared at her, my vision blurry, my legs weak, and my hands trembling. "Why are you telling me this?" I asked. "And why now?"

"He can't harm us here," my mother said. "And it is time you know the truth. So that . . ." She trailed off.

"So that what?"

"So that you don't turn into the kind of man he is," my mother said. "That is my biggest fear, and it is a fear I live with every day. That you will become a man like your father. I won't let that happen."

I leaned over and kissed her softly on the cheek and turned and began to walk away. "Where are you going?" my mother asked.

"Someplace quiet," I said. "Someplace where no one will see me."

"You needed to know," she said, as I started to walk along the sandy shore.

"And now I do," I said, turning back to face her.

"He's not a good man," my mother blurted out, practically shouting the words. "He's a bad man. A very bad man."

I SPENT THAT night on a quiet stretch of beach, watching the waves slap against the sand. I was filled with anger, rage, resentment, and fear. I couldn't process the fact that not only had my father taken someone's life—which would have been horrible enough on its own—but that he had taken the life of a woman he had sworn to love. How could he have done such an evil thing? And if he had killed one wife, what would stop him from killing a second, my own mother? And why did I have to be told here, on an island I had grown to love, in a place I finally felt was a home for me, a safe haven shielding me from all the darkness of my life in New York? I had no answers to any of these questions. I could only keep asking myself them over and over. I pictured my father taking me to ball games, to the park, for rides to Long Island to visit relatives. He laughed and joked with friends, then hid and cursed his fate when he got caught in a con or he owed too much to the loan sharks and couldn't pay them back. He would take me to movies and the circus, to boxing and wrestling matches, to concerts and amusement parks.

He was my father.

He was my friend.

And he was a murderer.

IT TOOK ME a few days before I could gather myself and visit Nonna. She knew my father before he married my mother, and I wanted—no, needed—to hear how she felt about him. She was sitting at the dining room table, the ever-present espresso pot by her side, a cup of coffee in her hand, when I walked into her home.

She waited for me to sit and silently poured me a cup of coffee. "You know about what my mother told me on the beach?"

Nonna nodded. "She thought you were old enough to know the truth," she said.

I took a sip of the strong coffee and looked across the table at Nonna. "Everyone thinks my father is a bad man. I've heard that since I was much younger. Even before I heard about him killing his own wife. That he's a bad man. They say it in the neighborhood where we live. And they say it here in Ischia. I hear it wherever I go."

"You can't stop people from talking," Nonna said. "That's what they do. Even if it's no business of theirs. There's no point listening to their words. Doesn't do you any good. What he is to them should mean nothing to you. What he is to you is all that matters."

"What do you think, Nonna?" I asked her. "What you think matters to me. Do you think my father is a bad man?"

Nonna stayed silent for a moment and then pushed her coffee cup away from her side of the table. "When my husband was in the hospital in Naples, sick from the disease that would take his life, we took turns spending the night with him. Some nights my daughters went, or my sons, and most nights I would go. Whoever went was given five lira to give to the nurse at the hospital to pay for the morphine that would help my husband make it through the night free of pain. This went on for many months. Your father was on the island during that time. One night he came to me and offered to go to Naples, give us a break from the long trip back and forth, a break from a night without sleep. I was grateful for his kind gesture and handed him the five lira and gave him the name of the nurse he needed to give it to."

Nonna pushed her chair back and stood, her eyes glancing up at the framed photo of my grandfather. "He came back the next morning and told me all went well," she said. "That night I went to the hospital to be with my husband. I saw the nurse and handed her the five lira. She told me my husband had been in a lot of pain the night before. I asked if the morphine wasn't working anymore. She told me my husband never got his morphine. She was never given the five lira. Instead, your father used that money to buy pizzas for himself and for some of the nurses. Your father ate pizza while my husband lay in a bed in a dark room filled with pain."

Nonna rested her hands on the table and looked at me. "Now, do you still want me to answer your question?" she asked. "Do you still want to know if I think your father is a bad man?"

I looked back at her and shook my head. "I'm sorry, Nonna," was all I could manage to say.

I pushed my chair back and walked slowly out of her house, not wanting her to see the tears I was shedding. I cried not just for the senseless murder my father had committed but for the pain he caused my Nonna, letting her husband, a man she loved her entire life, lay in a dark hospital room to endure a night of agony. It was yet one more thoughtless act committed by an uncaring man.

I hated my father now more than ever. He was not just a bad man but an evil one.

I hated him for what he had done to his first wife.

And I hated him just as much for what he had done to my Nonna. Both were acts that could never be forgiven.

SUMMER 1971

BY MY THIRD summer spent on Ischia, I felt even more at home on the island and with my mother's family. It was as if I were shielded within the confines of a warm embrace that kept me close and protected me from the family troubles back in New York. I felt that my family was collectively guiding me to a safer place, away from the problems caused by my father's debts and my mother's inability to calm his demons. For the first time, I had room to grow and dream and start to think about what a future for myself might look like. And, as expected, at the head of the loving pack of friends and relatives stood Nonna Maria.

I learned about life and forgiveness from her. About doing the right thing but on your own terms. She taught me to be determined, be focused, but never surrender to the easy out or turn your back on someone in need, even if that someone is a perceived enemy.

This last lesson Nonna had a lot of experience with. From the time my grandfather's younger sister, Nannella, learned of Nonna's love for Gabriel, she did little else but bad-mouth and torment her. She spread rumors with no basis in truth, yelled at her for no apparent reason, called her names, vilified her to all her friends. She did this throughout Nonna's marriage and continued it long after my grandfather died. No one understood the reasons for Nannella's hatred toward Nonna, and she ignored pleas from various family members to stop.

Through it all, throughout the years of gossip, innuendo, and hatred that was spewed forth by Nannella, my Nonna never said a word about it. Not in her own defense and not against her sister-in-law. She knew Gabriel had pleaded with his sister to bring the assaults to an end and asked him not to intervene. "Let her be," Nonna said. "Her words mean nothing to me."

Then, many years later, Nannella became sick. She was unwanted even by members of her family and was tossed from her home by her own children, whom she had also vilified through the years. She had no place to live, little in the way of money, and a damaged leg that needed constant medical care. Word got back to Nonna about her sister-in-law's situation. Nonna could have easily turned her back on the woman who had hurled such hatred at her for so many years. Instead, she asked her oldest daughter, my Aunt Frances, to find Nannella.

"My mother told me to let her know that the first floor of her house was empty and she could stay there for as long as she lived," Aunt Frances said to me. We were sitting on her terrace on Corso Vittoria Colonna, music from the restaurant behind her apartment building offering a comfort of its own. "Her meals would be brought to her, and Mama's doctor, her nephew, would tend to her bad leg. She would be charged nothing, not for the food, not for the room. But there was one condition."

"What was it?"

"That they never exchange a word between them," Aunt Frances said. "My mother would need to pass her room each time she went out of her home and each time she returned. But she wanted to hear not one word, not even a good morning. Not one single word. I found Nannella and passed on the message. She cried when she heard the offer and agreed. She moved in the next day and lived there until the day she died. And they never exchanged a single word."

Nannella was alive during the first three summers I visited the island. I would see her sitting in the entryway of her room each time I visited Nonna. She was a hunched-over old woman, sitting on a soft chair, her bad leg wrapped in bandages and resting on a stool. She always gave me a smile and asked me to say hello to Nonna as I went up the steps to see her. I did as I was told, but Nonna never budged, never acknowledged the greeting, and never asked me to pass one back.

I always wondered what made Nonna do what she did—take in a woman who had only ever acted hatefully toward her. Was it a simple act of kindness for a woman too old to care for herself? Had she forgiven her? Did she do what she did out of respect for my grandfather, believing it was something he would have done? Or was it more complicated than that? Was it a way for Nonna to show Nannella how wrong she had been about her? Or maybe it was simply the right thing to do. The only one who knew the real reasons she did what she did was Nonna, and, as was her way, she chose to lead by example rather than by explanation.

NONNA HAD A wonderful and expressive sense of humor, especially when she herself was the target. She spoke the dialect of Ischia, which is similar if slightly different in tone from that of Naples. But it's far removed from the proper Italian spoken on the streets of Milan, Florence, or Bologna. "A friend of mine came over to me this one time and was very upset," Nonna told me and my cousin Paolo one morning over a breakfast of fresh pastries and coffee. "She told me her son was about to make a terrible mistake. He had fallen in love with a young woman from Naples, and my friend was convinced the woman was a prostitute."

Nonna smiled and wiped at the corners of her mouth with a cloth napkin. "I had never heard that word before. It's not in our dialect. So I didn't know why my friend was so upset."

"What did you tell her?" Paolo asked.

"I told her the only thing that mattered was that the young woman didn't smoke," Nonna said with a laugh. "And my friend said, 'But, Maria, smoking or not smoking, she's still a prostitute.' I told her, 'There are some things you can't change.' "

"Did they get married?" I asked.

"Yes," Nonna said. "And they're still married, with three children of their own. It turns out my friend didn't understand what was said, either. The young woman wasn't a prostitute. She was a Protestant. But she found the man she loved and he found her. In the end, that's all that matters."

Nonna never went to church, rare for a woman of her generation living on an island where you can't walk more than a mile without passing the open doors of a Catholic church. She would happily sit in front of Saint Peter's but had not been inside for several decades. "I pray when I want and where I want," she told me when I asked why she never went to mass. "Doesn't have to be inside a church. But I'll be back in there soon enough."

"When?"

"For my funeral," she said.

Nonna found her refuge in her kitchen, standing in front of a hot stove, preparing large meals for the members of her family who ventured in and out of her home. In the summer months, her daughter Nancy and her husband, Benny, would stay with her, along with their two children, Paolo and Anna Maria. I would come for a meal at least three times a week, and my uncles, Mario and Joseph, would drop by whenever there was a break in their hectic tour schedules. A parade of cousins, grandchildren, and friends could always be counted on to stop in, usually during the hours when lunch was being served. And Nonna always made sure there was more than enough food to go around.

She excelled at the specialties of Ischia and Neapolitan cuisine, following each recipe by instinct instead of notes from a book. Her sauces were mostly fish- and vegetable-based and served over a bed of homemade pasta. She never served red meat but took pride in her chicken cacciatore and her wild rabbit sauce, for which the island has long been noted. She baked her own bread and had her wine delivered from the mountain vineyards of the D'Ambra family, friends of hers dating back to the World War II years.

My favorite of her meals was pasta puttanesca, a Neapolitan dish named in honor of the streetwalkers of that much maligned city. "Why is it called that, Nonna?" I asked as I stood against a wall of the kitchen, watching her prepare it for me for the first time.

"The sauce takes only ten minutes to make," Nonna said, "about the same time it takes to cook the pasta. Enough time for the ladies to enjoy a meal in between customers. Or so I was told. In Italy, there is a story behind everything, even a sauce as simple as this one." She looked over at me and smiled. "Grab an apron off the hook and come closer. I'll show you how to make it."

I wrapped an apron around my waist and stood next to her, watching as she placed a large pan on a front burner, the big pot with pasta water behind it coming to a full boil. "First you toss in the tomato sauce. I always use San Marzano tomatoes, because they make the thickest sauce. Then you toss in a couple of handfuls of capers, six or more sliced anchovies, depending on your preference, diced black olives, oregano, garlic, crushed red pepper, and olive oil. Stir it over a low flame. While you do that, I'll toss in the pasta."

"You don't add salt to the sauce?" I asked.

Nonna shook her head. "The anchovies give you all the salt you need. Too much and you'll be drinking water until the sun goes down."

"Who taught you how to cook?" I asked, watching her toss a kilo of pasta into the pot of boiling water.

"I learned same as anyone on the island learns," she said. "In Ischia, a girl learns to prepare a meal at an early age, especially if she's from a large family. Everyone has a job to do. Mine was to cook the meals. I passed on what I learned to my daughters. They took turns preparing the meals while I worked the store or went to Naples for supplies and my husband tended to his flock. And when they weren't making the meals, they worked the counter at the store and I cooked. I taught my sons to cook, too. Or they helped in the store or worked the fields. They weren't here just to eat. Everyone had to share in the work."

I kept stirring the sauce as Nonna drained the pasta. "Now comes the important part," she said. I watched as she tossed the cooked pasta back into the empty pot. She turned the gas burner off under the saucepan and looked at me. "Take that large spoon and start to lay the sauce on top of the pasta. Do it slow and easy and stir the sauce in as you're doing it."

As I was mixing the sauce with the pasta, I glanced over at Nonna and smiled. "Is this another story for me to write about?" I asked.

"No," she said, shaking her head and returning the smile. "This is what you eat after you finish writing the story. A good story is better if it's shared over a good meal and a glass of wine. I'll finish here. You go wait at the table. I'll bring out the plates and the glasses. While I do that, you think of a good story to tell. Make it one from America. A happy one. The only stories I've heard from America are from your mother, and they are never happy ones."

MY SUMMER MONTHS on Ischia weren't only white clouds and sunshine. A dark cloud always hung in the distance, waiting to bring me back to my life at home. I would get a sense of its arrival a few days before it would cross my path, the darkness making its presence known with either a letter or a phone call, signaling there was trouble brewing on the other side of the Atlantic. Trouble that always involved money and debts.

Nonna had lived a difficult enough life to also sense their dreaded arrival. You don't live through a world war, lose sons and grandsons during bombing raids, and see your husband wage a losing battle to an unbeatable disease without being aware of the darkness life often brings our way. She knew that no life was spared and always seemed ready for the next trial to come.

On this, my third summer on Ischia, trouble crossed my path on a late August day with a phone call from my mother. She always sounded frightened when she spoke on the phone, as if my father might rush in at any moment and yank it out of her hand. She was frantic, and her words were filled with panic. "The money," she shouted. "It's gone. All of it. It's all gone."

"What money?" I asked.

"Your school money," she said, her voice growing louder still. "The money to pay for you to go to school in September. He found it and took it all and now it's gone. There's not even a dollar left. You won't be able to go to school next month. I don't know what he did with it, but it doesn't matter. None of it is here. Not one penny."

I was attending high school at Mount Saint Michael Academy in the East Bronx. The tuition fee was sixty-five dollars a month. Each week, my mother and I would put aside the money I earned working a part-time job at a dry cleaner after school. We had thus far managed to keep up with the payments and hide the cash from my father.

Now my father had found my mother's hiding place, and the money was lost either at a racetrack, an OTB parlor, or in one of his latest bound-to-fail scams.

I did my best to calm my mother down and told her not to worry.

I would figure a way to earn the money and would pay the tuition on a month-by-month basis instead of sending in the complete amount at the start of the semester. I hung up the phone and stared out an open window, looking at the bay and an array of passing boats. I was in my Aunt Frances's kitchen, alone, and a light breeze brought some relief from the warm day.

I was flushed red with anger and resentment. I had already grown weary of the financial and emotional struggles my father put me through. With my mother's latest news came the gnawing and frustrating feeling that there would never be an end to it, that it would go on seemingly forever, that my father would always leave me scraping and scrounging for money, which he would so foolishly frivol away. I saw how if I wasn't careful, I would be trapped with him, trapped in my neighborhood and my life, without a chance to escape.

I began to think of not going back to New York, of making my home here, on Ischia, thousands of miles away from my father and the daily battle between him and my mother. I wanted to be free of them, able to choose my own path and find my own way in life, surrounded by people who loved me and actually cared about me. There was plenty of work to be had on the island, although I would probably never be a writer if I stayed. The main occupations revolved around the tourist trade or signing up for work on cargo ships. A writer's life never entered the equation. While my friends on the island read books and talked endlessly about the stories and authors they enjoyed, the very notion of making writing a career was considered beyond anyone's reach.

But I was willing to sacrifice that path for a shot at being happy. And in that moment, that seemed to me to be more than a fair trade-off.

There was another reason for my wanting to stay on the island. I was in love—or as in love as any sixteen-year-old could imagine himself to be. Her name was Francesca, and she was part of the small crew of friends I had made during my summers there. All the boys, from my cousin Paolo to my friends Gaspare and Pepe, had crushes on her, but from the very first moment I laid eyes on her, I was in love.

We met during my first summer on the island. I was fourteen that year and she was twelve. I was standing on the beach, being introduced to a long-standing family friend who I would soon discover was Francesca's mother. I felt a cold splash of water on my back, turned, and saw her for the first time. She was knee-deep in the water and smiled at me. "I'm going to swim out to that rowboat," she said, pointing at a boat that seemed to me to be quite a distance away. "Try to keep up, American. If you can swim, that is."

Her mother, Fernanda, smiled and patted me on the shoulder. "Give it your best," she said to me. "But I should warn you. She swims like a shark."

I never did catch her, but I did make it to the rowboat. From that day on, we met on the beach and swam, went to the movies, took long walks, and had pizza dinners, usually sitting on a stone wall on the Lido, facing the waters of the quiet bay. She, along with my friends, showed me the island they all loved so much. I fell in love with both—the island and the island girl—at the same time.

In the winters, we would write each other long letters once a week. I would write in Italian and she would respond in English, and I couldn't wait for the cold months to fade away and for the summer to arrive. I wanted to be with her forever, but I didn't know how I could manage that.

Her parents worked hard and were well off, living in a beautiful villa halfway between the port and the mountains. My parents were in constant debt, and any spare money I earned went toward that debt. We lived in a dank, dark basement apartment in the East Bronx, having moved out of Hell's Kitchen in the spring of 1969. The place was so small and uninviting that I dreaded the nights I spent there.

During my third summer on the island, I was sitting across from Nonna one late afternoon. We were quiet for several moments, each of us alone in our thoughts, finding comfort in the silence. "Coming here these past few summers has changed me," I said. "I've never felt so at home. I felt that way from the second I got off the boat. Like this was where I belonged."

"That's because it is where you belong," Nonna said. "This island is a part of you; it's as much in your blood as it is in mine. Nothing will ever change that. No matter where you go, where you end up, this place, this island, and the people you've met will always be a part of you. And that includes that young girl you care so much about."

I looked across at Nonna, and while my cheeks turned red, I couldn't hide the smile that crossed my face. "How do you know about that?" I asked.

"In Ischia, people like to talk almost as much as they like to go to the beach or for a late-night walk," Nonna said. "I've known her family forever. Her mother especially. If you ever go down to the beach and want to find her, look for the woman surrounded by children, making them all laugh with jokes and games. She has a great and giving heart."

"I like her a lot," I said. "She's almost like one of my aunts. And I think I'm in love with her daughter. I'm not sure. I've never been in love before."

"Does she feel the same about you?" Nonna asked.

"I've never asked her," I said. "I'm afraid she would say no. But I think she does."

I took a long sip of my now-cold coffee. "How did you know?" I asked. "With Nonno?"

"Sometimes a look is stronger than any word," Nonna said. "I took one look at him, he took an even longer look at me, and we both knew. I didn't need a second look, and neither did he."

"I'm as nervous about Francesca saying yes as I am about her saying no," I said. "A yes would make my heart jump out of my chest. But no would save her so much trouble."

"You're both still very young, and there's time," Nonna said.

"I know, Nonna," I said. "I have to finish school and figure out what to do after that. That's not what scares me."

"She's an island girl," Nonna said. "You live in a large city. And your mother and father cause you pain and worry. You're afraid to bring someone into that world."

"There's no escape," I said. "Every month, week, day, there's always something bad waiting. It's always going to be like that. I'm scared to bring her into that. That's probably why I haven't said anything to her."

Nonna poured herself a fresh cup of coffee and stared up at her husband's face. "All families have their dark side," she said. "A side they don't want anyone to see, a side they try to hide. My husband's family did not welcome me. They wanted nothing to do with me. His sisters, the one here and the one in America, never brought joy to our lives. In many ways, they brought ruin and heartbreak to my door. But we allowed nothing they did or tried to do to come between us. We ignored the slights and the insults—they were meaningless to us. And the more we ignored them, the angrier they got and the more vicious their verbal attacks. But we stayed strong."

"I don't know if I can do that, Nonna," I said. "I don't care if people don't like my father. You get used to that. But I do care that whenever we pay off one debt, there's another knock on the door and another man standing there telling me my father owes him money. That I can never get used to. It scares me and it scares my mother."

Nonna stayed quiet for several moments, gently stirring sugar into her cup of coffee. "It's a burden," Nonna said, glancing up at me. For the very first time I noticed a tone of sadness to her words, the harsh weight of her daughter's suffering coupled with my words of despair hitting her with a sudden force. "You're too young to have to deal with it, and your mother has seen enough dark days not to have to live through more. If you're looking for someone to blame for all that, then I'm the one you need to blame. It's my fault you both find yourselves in this position."

"How is any of it your fault?" I asked, not able to hide the surprised tone in my voice.

"I could have stepped in and stopped the marriage," Nonna said. "It was all arranged by your father's mother, who was my husband's sister in America. It would be a marriage between cousins. That alone should have been enough to prevent it. But my husband was dying, and your mother had been a widow for eight years and had a young son. And they were afraid of what the future would hold. The letter your grandmother wrote to my husband made many promises—of a better life with a man who would love and care for her. My husband was too sick to question it. He believed his sister. But I should have known better. I had heard their words before, and never once did I believe them."

"Why did you let it happen?"

Nonna shook her head. "I didn't," she said. "I allowed the sadness I felt watching the man I loved dying before my eyes to distract me from protecting my daughter from a man I knew would not be a good husband. But I want you to know I didn't know he had been in prison. I didn't know he had killed his first wife. None of us did. If we knew the truth, your mother would never have been allowed to marry your father. I would have rather died than let that happen. It is my fault. And I blame myself for it every day."

"My mother could have said no, Nonna," I said. "That would have been an easy thing to do. She didn't know him. I know she didn't love him. All she had to do was say no. I don't understand why she'd leave this beautiful place to marry someone she didn't love. That's not your fault."

"She believed the words your father told her," Nonna said. "He told her they would have a beautiful place to live and he had a good job with a great company. He promised he would send her son to the best schools. Your mother had been through a lot, losing a husband, a baby, and a brother in the war and then having to watch her father dying. She wanted to believe your father. She was looking for that better life. Maybe in her heart she knew it was a bundle of lies. But she willed herself to believe every word."

"Did Nonno live long enough to know the truth about my father?" I asked.

"He did," she said. "But by then your mother was pregnant with you and married to your father. They stayed on the island for a few months and we got to see the man he really was. Your father left for America a few weeks before my husband died. Your mother stayed behind to help us care for him. Nonno told her to stay here and raise the baby on the island. Here, he told her, she would be protected by family. That once she got on that boat and made the voyage to America, there was nothing any of us could do to help her."

"But still she went," I said.

"She was no longer her own woman," Nonna said. "She was now his wife. She left here eight and a half months pregnant, alone, to travel across an ocean, to a place she had never been to before."

"But my half brother stayed here," I said. "Living with you."

"For six years," Nonna said. "One broken promise among the many told by your father."

"It's not a happy story," I said. "And it's only going to get sadder."

"But it's one to remember and never forget," Nonna said. "Not all stories are happy ones. Most of them are tragic and filled with fear. No different than the life most people live day to day."

"I just wish I knew if the story ever ends," I said.

Nonna pushed her chair back, grabbed the coffeepot, and started to walk into the kitchen. "It will end like most stories," she said. "When somebody dies."

I found a level of comfort in Nonna's strong words. The lesson was a harsh one and it left its mark. It put into context my mother's plight and how the idea of an escape from her life was nothing more than a wasted wish. For her there was simply no way out.

But there was for me.

I was determined not to be a prisoner, forced to always step in and rescue my father from his troubles. I knew my escape would take time, months and years when I would still be shouldering his burden. But I would find a way to get out from under his thumb. And I would forge my own path, whether in America or on Ischia. I was determined to lead the life that would make Nonna proud, proof that her lessons had not gone unheeded. It would be a life of simple goals—to work for the money in my pockets and not take it from others. To care for any family that I might have. And to be everything that my father couldn't or wouldn't be.

To be an honest man.

IT WAS MY last night in Ischia for the summer. I went with Francesca and a group of our friends to La Terrazza for a pizza and white-wine dinner, and from there we bought a gelato at La Dolce Sosta and went for a long, quiet walk on the Lido. I had yet to tell Francesca how I felt about her, but I had a sense she knew without any words having to be exchanged. "I wish you could stay for a while longer," she said. We held hands as we walked, and the night sky was filled with stars. A warm breeze blew off the water, and the heavy heat of the day had slowly dissipated. I so wanted that walk to last forever.

"I don't want to leave," I said. "But I have to get back. School starts in less than a week, and I have to take care of a few things before I can go to class."

"You mean the money?"

I had told Francesca and my friends what happened back in New York with my tuition money. "I wish I had it to give to you," she said.

I looked at her and could only nod my thanks. In that moment, with her tanned face half covered by strands of long brown hair and her left arm brushing against my shoulder, I had never felt closer to anyone in my life. It's a moment that has been frozen in my mind.

"I'll be back next summer," I said to her. "I promise. And I'll keep writing letters every week. Even if my Italian is impossible to understand."

Francesca laughed and brushed the hair away from her face. "You're getting better," she said. "The more letters you write, the better you get."

"I finish high school next year," I said. "After that, I need to decide where I'll live and where I'll look for work."

"You talk about wanting to be a writer," Francesca said. "There aren't many of those here in Ischia."

I stopped and turned to face her. "But there's a lot here that is for me. Family, friends, and you," I said. "You're here. That matters to me."

"More than being a writer in America?"

"I don't even know if that's going to happen," I said. "The only one who seems convinced is Nonna. Everybody I mention it to back home laughs at the idea."

"That's because your Nonna believes in you," Francesca said. "If it's what you really want, you should at least try."

"You've read my letters," I said with a smile. "Do you think I could be a writer?"

Francesca laughed and brushed her right hand against my cheek. "Not if you write your stories in Italian," she said. "That would be a disaster."

"I don't even know what I would write about," I said. "Nonna says that there are great stories everywhere. All I need to do is listen."

We started walking again, the waters of the bay to our left, the lights of the large hotels on our right. "I heard one about your Nonna the other day," Francesca said. "My mother told me."

"What was it?"

"There's a man who keeps stopping her on the street, asking to buy her house," Francesca said. "He's asked her at least a dozen times all this summer. Each time, she walks past him without saying a word. The other day, he stood right in front of her, over by the barber shop on Via Roma. She looked up at him and he said, 'Signora, you would do me a great favor if you answered my question. Will you sell me your house?' "

"And what did Nonna say?"

"She stared right at him and said, 'And you would do me two favors if you never asked me that again.' Then she stepped around him and kept on her walk."

"She's got spine to her," I said. "She says what's in her heart, and she'll never lie to you. The only one who could get around her, persuade her to try something new, was my grandfather. He would do things that would normally make her angry, but she just couldn't be mad at him. My mother, my aunts, and my uncles talk about him all the time. It's almost as if he hasn't been dead for as long as I've been alive. I really wish I had a chance to meet him, even for a day."

"Did you hear the one about the winter clothes?" Francesca asked.

"I first heard it from my Aunt Nancy," I said. "She was working the counter at the store with my mother. It was getting close to the end of the summer season, and the weather was starting to change. A young woman walked in and was wearing a sweater similar to one my Aunt Nancy owned, one that Nonna had stored away with the rest of the winter clothes."

"Right," Francesca said, smiling. "The next day, your mother sees a woman wearing a jacket just like one she owned. That night, both your aunt and your mother asked Nonna when she was going to take the winter clothes out of storage."

"Little did they know that Nonna had been searching for those boxes for weeks and couldn't find them," I said.

"The way my mother tells it, your Nonna looks at your grandfather and asks him if he knows what happened to the winter clothes she stored away," Francesca said. "He reached over, held her hand, looked into her eyes, and smiled. He said to her, 'Maria, the people in the mountains have little or nothing at all. They need clothes for the winter. We have enough to buy clothes for the children. They don't.' "

"He gave all the clothes away," I said. "Didn't even think twice. To him it was not only the right thing to do, it was the only thing to do. Nonna just looked back at him and smiled. When she was telling my aunts and uncles what had happened to their clothes, all she said was, 'What are you going to do with a man like that except love him?' "

"Have you ever been to a funeral here?" Francesca asked.

I shook my head.

"The way they do it, they put the coffin in a horse-drawn black carriage," Francesca said. "The family walks behind the carriage. Any mourners wishing to show their respect walk behind the family. On the day of your grandfather's funeral, more than five hundred people showed up to march behind the carriage. No one here had ever seen anything like it."

"Who were they?"

"All the people he helped over the years," Francesca said. "The ones he gave clothes to. The ones he gave money to start a business. The ones he brought food and water to when they didn't have enough to feed their families. They cried for him as much as his own family did."

"Everyone says what a good man he was," I said. "And a lucky one. He had Nonna by his side."

"They had a great love for each other," Francesca said. "From the day he died, she still wears the widow's black. Most women here wear it for about a year, two at the most. Not her. She shows her love for him every day."

I looked over at Francesca. "Nonna says you know your true love when you see it," I said. "Do you believe that?"

Francesca wrapped her arms around my shoulders and rested her head against my neck. "Yes," she whispered. "I believe it."

NONNA CAME INTO the room while I was packing, and I turned to look at her. She had a pair of khakis folded across one of her arms. "I would like you to do me a favor," she said.

"Anything," I said.

She rested the khakis on the cot next to my suitcase. "I had the tailor up the road make these pants for you," she said. "I would like you to wear them on the flight home. Would you do that for me?"

"You didn't have to do that," I said.

"I know," she said. "They should fit you. He's the best tailor on the island."

"Thank you," I said. "Not just for the pants. For everything. Coming here, seeing you, being in Ischia every summer; it's all I think about when I'm in New York. Through the ugliest days, it's the one thing that keeps me going. Knowing I'll be back here. Even for just a few months."

"There will always be a place for you here," Nonna said. "Next year and in the years that follow. And you will always have a place to stay. Even when I'm no longer here."

I walked over and wrapped my arms around her. The idea of her dying was not something I had allowed myself to think about. I knew she was getting on in years, of course, but I thought of her as a superhero, letting nothing get in her way, not even illness or death.

Her nephew Agostino, the main doctor of the port area, checked on her regularly. He made Nonna one of his weekly house calls. Agostino was a brilliant physician and could have gone and practiced in any of the major cities of Northern Italy—from Milan to Bologna to Florence. Instead, he chose to come back to Ischia and care for the people he had known since he was a boy. I happened to be there one day during one of his visits. Nonna was always happy to see him, quick to pour him a cup of coffee from her always percolating pot. She brushed aside his questions about her health, keeping her focus on him instead. It was a routine they had perfected over the years. "You're always asking people how they feel," Nonna said to him. "But no one ever asks how you feel."

"I'm a doctor, Zia," he answered. Agostino was a short, thin, handsome man with a full head of white hair and a gentle manner. He was always well dressed and clearly loved his weekly back and forth with his favorite aunt. "I'm the one that's supposed to ask the questions."

"Well, with me you only need to ask one," Nonna said. "And I'm fine."

"You drink too much coffee," Agostino said. "And the way you take it would weaken the legs of a truck driver. Two sugars, if not three. Sometimes you melt a small piece of chocolate in with the coffee, along with a splash of Stock '84. That's why your blood pressure is high."

"I drink coffee the way I was taught to drink it," Nonna replied. "And I never drink coffee at night."

"Of course not," Agostino said with a laugh. "That's when you switch to white wine."

"It's good for the heart," Nonna said. "At least that's what I hear from other people."

"You never care what other people say," Agostino said. "Now suddenly you care."

"I only care if it's about wine," Nonna said.

Agostino reached into his medicine bag and took out a small bottle of pills. "I picked this up from the pharmacy on my way here," he said. "Take one a day. Nighttime would be better."

"What's it going to do to me?" Nonna asked.

"It will help control your blood pressure," Agostino said.

He looked over at me and asked if I would bring Nonna a glass of water. I headed toward the kitchen and stopped when I saw Nonna reach for the wine decanter in the center of the table. "I don't drink water," Nonna said. "I haven't had any since before the war. All the bombs, all the bodies left in the streets, turned the water brown and made it smell like medicine."

"But you make your coffee with bottled water," Agostino said. "If you can drink coffee, you can drink water."

"The water in my coffeepot gets boiled," Nonna said. "Kills all the germs. You're a doctor. You should know these things."

"I need you to take the pill, Zia," Agostino said. "One each day. Starting right now."

"In that case, you need to pour me a glass of wine," Nonna said.

I LOOKED UP at Nonna and waved goodbye, doing my best not to let her see me cry. She was standing at the top of the landing, her arms draped across the black railing, nodding as she watched me pick up my suitcase and begin my journey back to New York. I was wearing the khakis she had given me earlier in the day, and I took my time walking down the sloping hill toward the port and the hydrofoil that would take me to Naples. I passed the shop owners I had come to know, waving my goodbyes to them and taking in the sights and sounds of a place I had grown to love.

It was a long trip back, and I was happy that it was. It gave me time to think about what I was leaving behind and what I was about to face. I made my way to the boat and the eighteen-mile ride to Naples to the train station to Rome and then, finally, to Leonardo da Vinci Airport. It was all one big blur to me, and by the time I settled into my seat on the plane, Ischia felt very far away. Almost as if it had only existed in my dreams.

About halfway through the flight, I started to feel a pull against my left hip. I pressed a hand against the side of the khakis and noticed a bulge underneath the belt. I got up and went to the bathroom, slipping shut the door. I undid the belt and the pants and found a brown pouch sewn into the upper left-hand side of the khakis. I tugged at the pouch and yanked it free. There was money inside the pouch, American dollars. I took the cash out and counted it.

Down to the last dollar, it was the exact amount I needed to pay my high school tuition. Not just for a semester. But for a full year. I stood there stunned, spreading the money out in my hands. I lowered the toilet seat and sat down. I cried and smiled all at the same time. "Nonna," I whispered. "Nonna. My Nonna. My Nonna."

I pulled myself together, put the cash in my pocket, and made my way back to my seat. It was late afternoon when I got to the tiny apartment I shared with my parents, and they both seemed on edge. My mother hugged me, my father nodded at me, and that was as much of a welcome home as I could expect. But I didn't care. I needed to call Nonna. I needed to hear her voice.

I kept the money on me until late into the night, opening the pull-out bed in the middle of the living room, listening as my parents both fell fast asleep. I slipped the money under my pillow and waited until the sun came through the open blinds. I pretended to sleep as I heard my father leave early in the morning. My mother left a bit later, to attend her daily 9 A.M. mass at the local church.

I waited until I knew the mass had begun before I jumped out of bed and reached for the phone. It would be afternoon in Ischia, and as I dialed Nonna's number I knew she would be sitting at her dining room table, drinking a cup of espresso, enjoying the quiet of the day. She picked up on the third ring.

"Nonna," I said. "It's me. Lorenzo."

"You made it home safe," she said. "I'm glad."

"Nonna, I can't keep it," I said. "I love you for doing what you did. I love you more than you can imagine. But I can't keep the money. It belongs to you."

"What are you talking about?" Nonna asked. "What money?"

"What money?" I said. "The money you sewed into the pair of pants you gave me. The money to pay for my school. That money. I can't take it."

There was a quiet pause on her end of the line. Then Nonna said, "I don't know anything about any money. I bought you a pair of pants. If there was money in that pair of pants, then it's the tailor you need to thank. Not me."

"You had him sew the money in there," I said. "Into a pouch."

I heard Nonna laugh. It was a laugh I had come to know so well. A chuckle that came from deep in her chest, and once again I smiled through my tears. "I told you, didn't I?" Nonna said. "I told you he was a great tailor."

1975

ALTHOUGH I DIDN'T know it at the time, this was to be the last of my seven summers spent with Nonna.

I had first come to Ischia as a reluctant teenager, apprehensive about both the island and the relatives I would meet. In the intervening years, I had grown to love both, each finding a special place in my heart. I was close to my aunts, uncles, and cousins, and I had many friends on the island. I already knew nothing would ever bring an end to the affection we felt for one another.

NONNA WALKED INTO the kitchen and put a fresh pot of coffee on the stove.

"Have you been to Michelangelo's home, the one he built here on Ischia?" Nonna asked.

"Yes," I said, "a couple of times."

"He built it in such a way that from every window he could see the castle across the harbor," Nonna said. "He wasn't interested in the castle, but he was very interested in the woman who lived there in those years."

"Vittoria Colonna," I said. "She was his patron and she was a widow. There was nothing stopping him from having a romance with her. Unless what they say about him being gay is true."

Nonna shrugged. "I never listen to what people say," she said. "He was in love with her, and his love was so strong that even the great Michelangelo was too afraid to talk to her about how he felt.

When they did speak, they talked about art, other painters, the island, business affairs, and read poetry to each other. But he never talked to her about his love for her."

"How do you know all this?" I asked, smiling.

"My mother would take me past his house when I was little, and she would tell me the story of Michelangelo and Vittoria Colonna. They were the great loves of each other's life. And the love they had lasted until the day they died. It was never forgotten. And it's talked about until this very day, centuries later."

"Are you giving me another story to write about?" I said.

"A story and the lesson that comes with it," Nonna said. "A great love never goes away. It lives forever, maybe in silence, maybe only in your heart, and maybe you're the only one who knows about it. But it will always live. Maybe that's what you're destined to have with Francesca. If you leave this island with anything at all, leave here with that."

I never did tell Francesca how much I loved her. Nonna was right. The love I felt for her has lived on in silence and, across all these years, has never faded. But it can never be the same as it was during those seven glorious summers on Ischia. We remain perhaps what we were destined to be, friends separated by distant shores and different lives, cherishing memories from summers long since past. But Francesca will always remain my first true love. Nothing, not even the passage of decades, can ever bring those feelings to an end.

NONNA USED TO say even the clearest of skies can hide the darkest of clouds, bringing with it an unexpected storm. On the morning of August 5, 1975, on a warm and beautiful Ischia morning, one such cloud emerged, and an unexpected storm hit with a frightening and chilling fury.

I was walking toward Nonna's house, having left the family

building on Via Casciaro after spending the morning with a few of my younger cousins. It was ten minutes after eleven when I turned down the narrow landing leading to Nonna's home and was surprised to see dozens of men and women standing outside, some with handkerchiefs dabbing their eyes, all with sad and shocked expressions on their faces. I looked up toward the second floor and saw my Uncle Joe leaning on the black bars of the railing, his head down, crying.

I ran down the path and up the steps. Nonna's living room was filled with my relatives, all distraught, somber and worn.

As I made my way toward the couch against the far wall, I picked up snippets of dialogue. "A stroke," I heard one of my aunts say. "Agostino was here," another said. "All we can do is pray," a cousin said as I brushed past her. I was walking as if I were underwater, and the words barely registered. I squeezed my way through the small group edged around the couch and saw my cousin Paolo. He didn't say anything. He reached for me and hugged me, and we held each other for a long moment. When I finally let go, he stepped aside, and then I saw my Nonna.

She was lying on the couch, an oxygen tank to her right, two air tubes in her nose, her face distorted, her eyes closed. Her breathing was labored, and she could only take breaths through an open mouth. I got on my knees and reached for her hand and held it. It was cold and limp. I looked up and saw my Aunt Nancy. She was wiping tears from her eyes and shook her head. "There is nothing for us to do," she managed to say. "She can't be saved."

I leaned up and rested my head on Nonna's left shoulder, my lips close to her ear. "Nonna, please," I whispered. "Please, don't die. Not now. Not today. Please."

I stayed there for the longest time, clutching her hand tighter and tighter, my eyes closed, listening to her breath, now coming in rapid spurts. I heard a long, slow rattle in her throat. And then, nothing. I lifted my head and looked at her. Her mouth was closed, her head tilted to one side, her chest still.

I caressed her hair and kissed her on the forehead. Behind me, I heard the cries and wails of her children and grandchildren, of her friends and family. They were all distant echoes to me. I stayed there on my knees, my hands touching her white hair, staring at the old woman I had come to love and cherish across seven summers. A woman who had first met me as a teenager and was now leaving me as a young man. I loved every day I spent in her company, and I knew, even at that saddest of moments, there would never be anyone like her in my life.

One of my uncles reached for me and gently pulled me away. "They need to prepare her for burial," he said in a soft voice. "Come wait outside with me."

I got up, and we weaved our way through the sad faces and walked to the landing. We stood there, neither of us saying a word. He had just lost his mother. I had lost my guiding light.

In Ischia, burial has to be within twenty-four hours. A mass at Saint Peter's Church was quickly arranged, and the cemetery was alerted. I made my way down the stairs and stood against a stone wall and watched as men from the church came and went. Paolo came up next to me. "It shouldn't be a shock when an old person dies," he said. "But somehow it always is."

"That's because we never thought of Nonna as old," I said. "She lived and acted as if she would be around forever. And there was a part of me that believed she would."

"She wasn't afraid of it," Paolo said. "But, then, she wasn't much afraid of anything."

"What happens now?" I asked.

"After the mass, we go to the cemetery, and she'll be buried before sundown," Paolo said. "That's temporary. After two years, her remains will be moved to the family vault, and she will be laid to rest next to her husband."

"Together again," I said.

Paolo turned to look at me and managed a weak smile. "To be honest, I don't think they've ever been apart. Nothing, not even death, could separate them."

"And she brought us together," I said. "Gave me a family and friends to love. I don't know what I would have been like if I hadn't met her."

"There's time for us to go get a coffee before we need to be at the funeral mass," Paolo said.

I smiled for the first time that day. "I think that's something Nonna would love for us to do," I said.

"The coffee won't be as good as hers," Paolo said. "And it won't be as strong."

"No, it won't," I said. "And it won't ever be again."

THE CHURCH WAS as crowded as I'd ever seen it and the funeral procession even more so. It was a final chance to say goodbye to Nonna, not just for me but for everyone—the friends she had helped start in business; the ones still remembering the kindness of my grandfather; the friends who had stood by her side during good times and bad; family members who she loved and cared for. They all came, stopping at the entrance to the cemetery, with heads bowed, paying their final respects to a woman who gave them all so much to remember.

My Nonna died on that day, August 5, 1975.

But in my heart and in my mind, she never left us. She is always with me, each and every day. She is a part of me, and she will never leave my side.

I have tried to live up to the man I believe Nonna wanted me to be. I have not always succeeded, failing more times than I care to admit. But I did not become a man like my father. I married a woman I loved and respected, and together we raised two children Nonna would have been happy to know.

And, yes, Nonna, thanks to your many stories, I somehow found my way and made a living as a writer.

RAFFAELA

1939 – 1954

❧

MY MOTHER WAS still a teenager when she met the love of her life. His name was Mario Scubla and he was a carabiniere from the region of Udine in Northern Italy, stationed briefly on the island of Ischia. She was a happy young woman in those years, surrounded by a tight-knit family and close friends. And meeting the handsome young officer only made her happier.

During my summers in Ischia, my aunts and uncles would often tell me stories about my mother—playing practical jokes on her brothers and sisters, always with a smile on her face, eager to greet the new day. In their stories, she was the first to share a funny joke or make a meal for a sick friend. She loved going to the movies and working in the family store. She was very religious, and that only added to her contentment.

My mother was eighteen when she first married, and soon after, her husband was transferred back home to Udine. There they bought a parcel of property and began to build a home and start a family. My mother loved every minute of her time there. "The weather was colder than I was used to in Ischia," she would tell me. "And the food was more meat oriented than fish, but the people were warm and friendly and they took me in as one of their own. Those few years spent there were the happiest ones of my life."

They were married for six years and had two children, both sons. "I would get up before the sun rose," she would say, "feed the children, and have breakfast with my husband. He would then head off to work and I would supervise the building of our home. My sister Anna came up from Ischia to be with me. She was still single and grew to love the area and the people as much as I did. It was a wonderful time, and I had no reason to think it wouldn't always stay that way."

On his days off, her husband would help her with the children, organize family outings, and help choose furniture for the home they looked forward to sharing together. He treated her with kindness and affection, reaching for her hand when they went out for an evening walk and smiling at the stories she told about the children and how she and her sister had impressed the building crew by showing up at the work site before they did. "We were very much in love," she told me. "My life with him and our children was everything I imagined it would be, and we were still both so young. Such a shame it had to end. We never did get to see our house finished."

For my mother, those blissful days were not meant to last. In short order, she would learn the harsh lesson that, for her, happiness would exist only as a memory.

During the dark days of World War II, my mother's husband was transferred to Salerno, in Southern Italy. The city was under relentless bombings from both Allied and Nazi planes. Nightly air raids were as common as sunsets, and residents had to learn to make do without fresh milk for their children and bread and meat for their dinner tables. By this time, my mother had a two-year-old son and a six-month-old infant.

For the first time in her life, my mother experienced the ugly grasp of fear, and, sadly, it would keep its hold on her for the rest of her life.

During those horrible months, her husband became ill with a disease that has never been fully explained to me. Whatever it was, it sapped him of his strength and would, in a matter of months, take his life.

Within weeks of her young husband's funeral, my mother endured a second tragedy: Her six-month-old baby died.

Again, she never spoke about the specifics of his death; it was far too painful a subject. From what she did say, I gathered that my half brother died during a bombing raid on Salerno, already sickly due to the fact my mother could no longer breastfeed him and was keeping him alive with milk from other young mothers in the area.

In a very short span, my mother suffered two heart-crushing losses—her husband and her infant son. She was a widow living in a bombed-out city with a two-year-old boy and very little in the way of money or food.

She was not yet twenty-four years old.

I WOULD HAVE loved to meet the happy version of my mother. The young woman who was quick to smile and full of life and joy. That young woman remains a mystery to me.

I only knew the one who had been beaten down by the sadness of a first marriage that ended in death and a second that caused a fog of despair, debt, and dread. With my father, she was a prisoner in a cell without bars, following him from one shabby apartment to another, haunted always by his shadow and the tentacles of a family that never left her alone.

While I was growing up, there were many days when I resented my mother. I was angered by her willingness to shroud herself in victimhood and what I saw as her inability to stand up for herself and forge her own way out of her daily hell—whether with or without me. But over time I have come to understand that it takes an enormous amount of inner strength to withstand the daily abuse, both physical and emotional, she experienced at the hands of my father. It takes a courage that few have and even fewer can sustain. It takes bravery and a will to survive it all, when it would be easier to surrender.

My mother never surrendered. Not one single time.

SOON AFTER THE war ended, my mother moved back to Ischia to live with her family, a widow now with a young son. She would wear the widow's black for eight years. Even though the war was over, the people of Ischia struggled to rebuild the life they had once known. Food was still in short supply, work was difficult to come by, and there were warnings not to drink the water, polluted by the bombings during the war.

There was an air of sadness around my mother during those years, her only comfort found in the company of family and friends. She had no intention of getting remarried and rebuffed any attempts by the locals who would get up the nerve to ask her out for an evening walk. "I had my son," she told me. "I had my family. And I had my memories of happier times. I didn't need anything more than that."

For those eight years, my mother led a quiet but serene existence. Her world was built around family, her son, church, a few friends, and quiet walks on empty beaches. It was a peaceful life and one she fully embraced.

Then, once again, life intervened.

Though this time not in any way that brought her happiness. In the autumn of 1953, my Nonno Gabriel, my mother's father, was diagnosed with cancer. Nonna and their children were devastated. For so many years, he had been the center of their life, the anchor each one depended on. But his disease quickly overwhelmed his body, and there was little to do other than give him daily doses of morphine, both in the hospital and at home, to help ease his pain. My grandfather was given six months at most to live.

It was during this time, close to the end of his life, that the letter from America arrived. It would be a letter that would change the course of my mother's life. It was written by my grandfather's sister, an aunt my mother had never met, and it was addressed to her dying brother. In a dozen or so paragraphs, her words were read aloud to him, words that extolled the virtues of her son, Mario. He was described as a caring, loving, and hardworking man who would make a perfect husband for Gabriel's widowed daughter. She stressed that Mario, too, had suffered a great loss—the death of his first wife—so a common bond already existed between the two. My grandfather was taken in by his sister's words and her concerns for his daughter. He was too weak to question it, too drugged to see the lies hidden behind her words. My grandmother had her doubts. She had little reason to believe anything her husband's family said, but she, too, was in a weakened condition, forced to sit by and watch the only man she ever loved dying before her eyes.

The letter was a scam. It failed to mention that the loss of her son's wife was not caused by illness or accident. She was murdered, suffocated with a pillow in a cheap Manhattan hotel room. She didn't write that he was convicted of second-degree manslaughter and had only recently been released after serving seven and a half years in prison.

There was not a word about his gambling habits or his inability to hold down a steady job. She didn't tell them he was a wife beater, a con man, a liar, and a serial womanizer. She ignored the fact that she was proposing a marriage between two first cousins.

My grandfather remembered meeting my father when he had first visited Ischia in 1938 and that he seemed to be a decent young man. He sat my mother down and told her this marriage would give her a second chance to have a good life, to live in a country that offered great promise, with a man who would be a husband to her and a father to her young son. My mother was reluctant to marry a man she didn't even know, but she heeded her father's words. She also realized that her son, now almost twelve, did not seem cut out for a life in Ischia, where he had fewer opportunities for education and a career than he would in America. The boy was quiet, shy, had few friends, but was very studious and intelligent. She had heard stories of the few islanders who had left for America and found great fortune on its shores. She thought the same could be true for her son, as well.

My father arrived on Ischia in late November 1953, and the marriage was set for mid-January of the following year. In the few months before his marriage, my father was on his best behavior, courting my mother and telling my ailing grandfather and anyone else within earshot about the large apartment he had rented for his daughter and her son to live in and the great job he had managing a meat-market company that supplied beef to the top restaurants in New York City. My father was an excellent con man and had them all convinced that my mother and her son were on their way to a better life.

My parents were married on January 18, 1954. They honeymooned in Pompeii and it was there, on their first night together, that my father told my mother the truth about his first wife. "He told me in such a calm way," my mother told me years later. "He said it wasn't his fault. His wife had told him she was in love with another man and he couldn't just let her go. A wife stays with her husband. It's where she belongs. That's when I knew that I was not going to any land of great promise. I was going to a prison of my own making."

They returned to Ischia, and my mother soon learned she was pregnant with me. My father, now married and soon to be a father, tossed aside his kind façade and reverted to what he truly was. He was short-tempered and quick to place blame on those closest to him. He began to borrow money from family friends and gamble it away betting on the local numbers. He cheated on my mother with a woman who owned a dress shop and didn't know he was a married man. He then told my mother that maybe it would be best for her son to stay in Ischia, at least for a while, until she got settled in New York. That short stay would last for six years.

My grandfather, inching closer to death's door by the day, realized the mistake he had made. He sat my mother down and pleaded with her to stay in Ischia, have her baby there, and not go to America with a man who could not be trusted. She would be protected by her family, and a way out of the marriage could be found.

"I couldn't put my family through that," my mother would tell me many years later. "I couldn't put them through the shame and scandal that would cause. I was the one who had made the mistake, and I was the one who had to deal with what came with that mistake."

My father left the island late in the spring of 1954 to go back to New York to prepare for the arrival of his new bride and their child. He told them he had to get back to his job, though he had worked only one part-time job since his release from prison and had limited prospects at finding work that paid enough to support a family.

My mother stayed behind, spending her days by her father's side, both of them consumed by the grave mistake they had made. "I am so sorry, little one," my grandfather said to her one late afternoon, his voice barely above a whisper. "I'm the one that is to blame for the life that waits for you with this man, but you will be the one that has to suffer. That causes me more pain than you can imagine."

Soon after, on August 13, 1954, my grandfather, Gabriel Carcaterra, took his final breath.

1954–1960

MY MOTHER ARRIVED in New York City in mid-September 1954. She was expecting to move into a beautiful three-bedroom apartment in an upscale part of Manhattan, which my father had described to her in detail. Instead, her first New York apartment was in a run-down tenement with no hot water, a bathtub just off the small kitchen, and a bathroom out in the hall, shared by the other three families living on the floor. One of my only memories of that apartment is of sitting in the bathtub, the large butcher block used to cover it spread out sideways with a bowl of macaroni resting in the center for me to eat.

The area where we lived was one large strip of tenements, and the residents were all Italian. That first building was on West 67th Street, in the area now occupied by Lincoln Center. The locals who lived in the neighborhood called it Little Naples, since most of the residents were from that southern city or its adjoining islands.

The rent was paid in cash, and what little heat there was in winter was turned off at 10 P.M. and turned back on at 6 A.M. When it was cold, the windows were covered with ice. Many a long, frigid night was spent huddled together in the kitchen, the oven door open, the gas on full volume, me in my mother's arms, wool stockings on her feet.

The summers were even worse. The rooms were so hot you had trouble catching your breath. The windows provided no relief, and any fans we could afford blew hot, humid air. The clothes we wore were soon drenched with sweat, and the only break from the brutal heat was to sit on the front stoop, hoping to catch a breeze from the river, two avenues down.

As soon as I was old enough to sit up, my father would place me in the street, alongside the curb, the cold water from an open fire hydrant rushing against my bare legs and chest, a small toy boat in my hand. He would smile down at me and rub cold water on top of my head and, on the nights when he had some extra money in his pockets, splurge and buy me and my mother ice cones from the man working the stand on the corner.

I was born a few weeks after my mother's arrival in New York, on a Saturday afternoon in mid-October at Saint Clare's Hospital, on West 51st Street in Hell's Kitchen, an area that would become our home after the tenements were razed.

My mother was forced to live surrounded by people speaking English, a language she did not understand, who did not treat her arrival with warmth but instead regarded her as an interloper thrust into their lives. Whatever love or attention that was shown was focused solely on me, my father's son and the family's golden child. This caused her to bury herself deeper into her silent shell. My father's family felt free to talk about her in her presence, knowing full well she would have no idea what they were saying, although she knew from their smiles and facial expressions that the words spoken were not kind ones. And when her new family members did make attempts to speak Italian, theirs was a bizarre hybrid, a mixture of Ischia dialect picked up from their mother and Americanized Italian words that only caused confusion.

"It was as if I was invisible," my mother would tell me in later years. "Your father would pull some scam, one that cost us money we didn't have, and they would sit around the table and laugh about it. In front of me. And during the few months a year when your father did work and we managed to set aside some money, they would find out about it—usually from him, since he told his mother everything about us. Soon enough, one of them would be knocking on our door, looking for a loan. And your father was quick to give it to them. Having his family so close to us, his mother living next door, was unbearable. I would look around that apartment and wonder what awful crime I had committed to be put in such a place."

My mother was not just ignored, she was ridiculed. As I grew older, I was made an accomplice in that ridicule. Looking back on it now, all these years later, the thought still makes me shudder in shame.

My father's mother lived next door to us during our six years in Little Naples. She was a stout, domineering woman with total control over her out-of-control son. My father, for all his street toughness and macho appearance, was at heart a mama's boy and did all he could to please his mother. She was quick to make excuses for his mistakes, even going so far as to spread vicious and unfounded rumors about the woman he killed. She would start feuds between close friends by making up gossip and was known to lend money out on the street in return for a quick profit. My father would visit her practically every day and would take her advice on any matter, even when it caused damage to our own family. And when he lashed out at my mother physically, his mother would be the first to come to his defense and sit with my mother, nurse her wounds, and tell her she needed to be a more understanding and loving wife.

"There were many days and even more nights when I thought the best way for me to get out was to kill myself," my mother told me a few years after we had moved from Little Naples to Hell's Kitchen. "But, then, that meant leaving you to them, and that I couldn't do. They would have ruined you and you would have turned out to be just like them. You would have made nothing of your life. So, instead, I lived. For you and for the son I had in Italy."

MY FATHER'S FAMILY taught me to curse in Italian. They found it funny to have a young boy stand in front of complete strangers and toss an array of Neapolitan curse words in their direction. It was a routine that became quite common whenever company arrived at my grandmother's apartment. I would be placed in the center of the living room and prompted to hurl foul language at the faces assembled around me. The laughter was loud and immediate, and I delighted in the attention. But then I would glance over at my mother, usually standing off in a corner of the room, and see the sadness etched across her face. I was too young to know that what I was doing was wrong and much too young to realize that the words that caused others to laugh and burst into applause brought only shame and humiliation to my mother.

If it ended there, if all I was taught was to curse in Italian to entertain strangers, then my father's family's behavior could be written off as juvenile and relatively harmless. But they were not content to stop there—they had to take their mockery of my mother a step further.

They taught me to call her by her name, Raffaela. Or, even worse, their Americanized version of it, Filene. Not Mom. Not Mama. Not Mommy. But Raffaela or Filene. This was humiliating to my mother. In Italy, no son ever calls his mother by her given name, especially as a child. It is a sign of disrespect, a diminishing of her status as a mother. All those times, in front of all those people, when I would call her by her name or its silly Americanization, caused her a great deal of pain. When it became too difficult for her to bear, she would leave the room, her eyes moist with tears, turning her back on the cruel laughter of people she had grown to despise.

My mother would correct me when we were alone together, further shamed by having to explain that she was my mother and I should call her by that name. And it would work; I would call her Mom. At least until the relatives visited and the spectacle of calling her by her given name started all over again. Their laughter, their mocking of my mother, caused a gulf between the two of us. It made my mother despair even more about the situation she found herself living in, with even her own son now turned against her. She was alone and friendless during those years, and looking back I realize I contributed to those feelings. She was alienated, and I made her feel even more so. At the time I was too young to understand what was happening, and by the time I realized the effect it had on her, the damage had already been done.

MY PARENTS FOUGHT constantly, usually over money, of which there was very little. My father worked sporadically, gambled incessantly, and was always thinking up ways to con working people out of their earnings. If my mother's complaints became annoying to him or if she spoke to him when he was in one of his dark moods, then he would lash out at her.

And if I happened to get in the way, I would be hit just as hard as she was, regardless of how young or defenseless I might have been. My father was a bull of a man—five foot seven inches tall, two hundred forty pounds of pure muscle. He had been a boxer in his youth, a destructive punching machine who never lost an amateur bout.

My mother was in a loveless marriage, wed to a hot-tempered, violent man who had served seven and a half years in prison.

She was surrounded by family members who coddled him, shrugged away his indiscretions and abuse, and left my mother alone, in a city where she knew no one, couldn't speak the language, and could only find solace when she went to church and prayed.

This was my mother's world.

This was her prison sentence.

A nightmare without an end.

1961–1969

〜✦〜

SHORTLY BEFORE THE bulldozers destroyed the tenements, we moved to Hell's Kitchen. The building at 532 West 50th Street was owned by a genial Italian couple, Frank and Kate Antonelli. The building was well maintained, and the apartment was a railroad one, much larger than the one we had lived in for the previous six years. Even better, none of my father's relatives were within striking distance.

Mrs. Antonelli would become my mother's first close friend in America, someone she could talk to, share her problems with, and even, on rare occasions, reminisce with about happier days spent in her home country. My father had, for a few months at least, put his focus on work and was bringing home a steady paycheck for the first time since he married my mother. I was sent to the local Catholic school, where two of the nuns—Sister Josephine and Sister Timothy—spent endless hours teaching me to speak English. We were, for the moment, a working-class family at peace.

Then my half brother, Anthony, arrived from Italy, and the problems that had been buried beneath the surface came boiling to the top, and the daily battles began anew.

My mother was clearly thrilled to have her son living with her. He was seventeen, tall, lanky, shy, spoke some English, and was doted on by my mother from the time he walked into the apartment. She prepared his favorite meals, peppered him with an endless series of questions about family members back in Ischia, and was eager to see him enrolled in the local Catholic high school, Power Memorial.

Throughout this period, my father was cordial to his stepson and at times even encouraging. He laid down some early ground rules, among them being that he needed to find a part-time job. "There are no free rides here, kid," my father told him. "Everybody has to carry their weight, and that includes you."

Anthony quickly found an after-school job at a supermarket on Ninth Avenue, earning pocket money for himself and table money to contribute toward the family expenses. But still my father wasn't satisfied. Beneath the surface, he was seething with anger at both my mother and her son, and it was only a question of time before he found a reason to lash out. My mother could feel the rising tension and did her best to shield her son from it.

But, in the end, it all proved to be a waste of time. My father was going to do what he was born to do—cause havoc and pain—and my mother, as always, would be unable to prevent any of it from happening.

I have no memory of what caused my half brother to be kicked out of the apartment the first time. I asked my mother a number of times, and my questions were ignored. Asking my father only led to my getting yelled at and being told to "mind your own business and keep your trap shut, unless you want to be tossed on your ass like that bum."

That first eviction led to a revolving door of my half brother living with us for a short time, getting tossed out of the apartment, living in places known only to my mother, and then moving back in with us again. It was during these long, frustrating years that I could see my mother's behavior toward me shift. She would often glare at me in silence, seeing the image of her hated husband in my face and eyes. She would fret over my half brother's living situation and always referred to him as "my son," a phrase that she no longer applied to me. My half brother was her son and I was my father's, and in her mind that's how it would always remain.

I resembled my father in both appearance and gestures, and in my early years I was closer to him than I was to my mother. I would read the daily newspapers to him when he came home from work, starting from back to front, sports to the news. He would interrupt on occasion and share stories of his favorite boxers and some of his own bouts in the ring. While I sat with him in one room, my mother was huddled away in the kitchen, listening to Italian religious programming on the small battery-operated radio she kept on the counter, her fingers wrapped around a set of rosary beads, praying for an end to her misery.

As I got older, my mother buried herself deeper into her shell of despair, emerging only sporadically to enjoy time in the company of Mrs. Antonelli, go to mass, or visit with her son, visits that needed to be kept secret from my father for fear of the anger they would provoke.

There were several times when the beatings were so severe my mother needed to be taken to Saint Clare's Hospital. On some of those occasions, I was caught in the middle of my father's vicious assaults and found myself in the hospital alongside her, both of us waiting to have our wounds stitched. The nuns working in the hospital were used to these visits. Not just from us. Spousal abuse was common in those days in that neighborhood. There were no social workers to file a complaint with, no cops poking around to ask us who caused the welts and the cuts, no relatives we could turn to for help or relief. In that war, back in that time, my mother and I were left to fend for ourselves.

The beatings I endured at my father's hand did not change my feelings toward him. He was capable of administering a beating in the afternoon if I came home with a bad grade on a test and then, less than two hours later, taking me on the subway to a twi-night doubleheader at Yankee Stadium, splurging on hot dogs and Cracker Jacks and a long night of baseball, both of us happy and content. It became bearable to accept that this was the way of our life.

The beatings my mother endured were another matter. I would sometimes get angry with her for pushing him, nagging him, until he exploded with uncontained fury. Other times, I felt helpless over my inability to do more to protect her. One time, I stepped in between the two, a meek attempt to stop the beating. My father glared at me. "You little punk," he said. "You picking her over me? Over your own father? I'll throw you out that fucking window if you even think of doing that again."

My mother would talk to herself most days, build her anger into a frenzy so that by the time my father came through the apartment door, she would vent the full fury of her frustrations at him. I would beg her to stop, but she always ignored me. And there were many times when I felt a hateful rage for her that should have been directed toward my father. I felt sorry for her most times and terrified for her during the worst of the beatings. I also often wondered why she simply didn't pick up and leave. Take my half brother and return to Ischia. If, as she always said, Anthony was her son and I was my father's, then I didn't think my father would have cared very much if they were both out of his life.

It was at this time, around my tenth birthday, that the anger and frustration my mother felt about her plight and her inability to do anything about it found an outlet. Someone to whom she could vent and air her feelings, give a release to the hatred in her heart, and attack without fear of retribution. She aimed her venom at me.

The first time it was unleashed, it caught me off guard and caused

me a great deal of confusion and sorrow. Over the years it continued, and I grew to understand that I was merely a stand-in, an
opportunity for her to say what was truly in her heart, regardless of
how hurtful, without risking a beating. Initially, I resented the verbal attacks and the slights. But over time I turned her negativity
toward me into motivation to prove her wrong, to make her see that
I would not be the same man my father was.

I remember we were sitting in the kitchen of our Hell's Kitchen
apartment the first time she verbally attacked me. It was closing in
on Christmas, and my mother was holding a stack of bills that
needed to be paid with money we did not have. My father always
chose the holidays to set off on a destructive course and we were,
once again, buried in debt.

My mother looked up from the bills and across at me. I was standing with my back to the small refrigerator, my fingers wrapped
around a cup of warm cocoa. She glared at me, and then the words
came out in a loud, high-pitched voice: "If only you were born
dead," she said, "none of this would have happened. If you had been
born dead, I would have my life back. I would be with my family,
back in Ischia, and not stuck here in this prison. I would have my
son with me, and we would both be happy. Instead, I'm here and I'll
be here for as long as he lets me live. All because of you."

My mother had never spoken to me in that way before, and the
words hit me so hard they took my breath away. I always knew she
preferred my half brother to me, and I had come to accept it. But
wishing me dead was not something I had ever expected to hear
from my mother. I was the one who took her to the hospital, who
helped nurse her wounds, who listened to her litany of laments. I
was the one she always turned to after the latest onslaught from my
father. My half brother, her son, was never around during those
troubled times.

"I didn't do anything" was all I could say.

"You lived," she said, practically spitting out the words. "You lived, and because you lived I don't get to see my son and I don't get to see my family. I have to live here with you and with him. Those are the faces I see. I pray every day that the Good Lord takes you both so I can be free again."

I stepped away from the refrigerator and rested my cup of cocoa on the stove top. I turned and walked to the door leading out of the apartment. I opened it and looked back at my mother. "I'm sorry," I said. I then walked out of the apartment, letting the door slam closed behind me.

OUR DAYS TOGETHER weren't always shrouded in darkness and hate. My mother was an excellent storyteller when the mood suited her. Her reading was limited to *Il Progresso*, the Italian-language daily, and religious newsletters given out by our local church. But on winter Sunday afternoons she would take me to a small theater in the neighborhood, which put on short Italian plays followed by an Italian movie. The movies were in black and white and shown without subtitles. And those Sunday afternoons served as my first introduction to Italian neorealism and the harsh reality lived not only by my mother but by most of the women in attendance.

I was mesmerized by the movies—from Roberto Rossellini's *Rome Open City* to the early works of Federico Fellini—and by the artistry of the legendary Italian comic Totò. But most of all I was overwhelmed by the sheer power and artistry of Vittorio De Sica, who remains to this day my favorite film director. I watched *Bicycle Thieves* and *Two Women* and *Umberto D.* in stunned silence. I would sit with hands folded on my lap, completely enthralled with the story, the characters, the dialogue, and the visualization of the brutality of life. It was storytelling in its purest and most honest form.

These were not the sugarcoated war movies I saw on American television sets, usually with John Wayne in the heroic role. If those movies showed Italians at all, we were either cowards, traitors, or villains. Here, instead, in these gut-wrenching and honest films, we suffered with dignity and courage and a fierce determination to live despite the odds.

When on rare occasions a comedy was shown, like De Sica's *Marriage Italian Style*, I took pleasure in a story well told. The characters in those movies shared the ability to laugh at the obstacles in their paths and were able to talk themselves out of any situation, no matter how complicated.

The lessons I learned on those Sunday afternoons, sitting next to my mother, watching and listening to stories about a people and a place far from the one I knew, further fueled my desire to one day tell stories of my own. I still did not know how that would be accomplished, or even if it could, but the seed had been planted.

Those long afternoons were when I felt closest to my mother and were some of the happiest and also saddest times we spent together. Those films went a long way toward helping me understand the life my mother had led and the life she had left. She had suffered through a world war. Lost a husband, a baby, and a nineteen-year-old brother. That should have been enough suffering for one lifetime. Instead, she survived that war only to be thrust into another. One even deadlier and more unrelenting than the one she had left behind. On those Sundays I fully grasped why my mother so hated her life in America.

After the show, the women in attendance would sit quietly, dry their tears, and then a handful would begin to share their thoughts, observations, and, most important of all to me, their stories. My mother, usually silent and afraid to speak in public, here finally felt free enough to share some anecdotes from her life.

"The sound of a bomb exploding close to you stays with you forever," my mother said to the group one afternoon. "You never hear it coming—at least I didn't. You just see the ground around you destroyed and then you smell the smoke and you hear the cries for help for the dead or dying. And all you can do is grab your children and run, but you never know which is the best way to go. Because you never know when and where the next bomb is going to fall."

Some of the women around us shifted their seats closer to where we were. While my mother spoke, the elderly man who ran the theater handed out paper cups filled with espresso and left a small platter of biscotti on an empty seat. He then sat and listened along with the gathered women and their children.

"I was running once during a bombing raid in Salerno," my mother said, tears welling in the corners of her eyes. "I remember I had lost a shoe somehow, tripping over a rock maybe. The smoke was thick, and it burned to breathe. I was holding my baby in one arm and had my oldest by the hand. You don't think about living or dying in a moment like that. You only think about taking the next step and then the next one."

"And you feel as if the bombs will never stop falling," one of the women sitting next to my mother said. "You feel as though you will have to run forever, even though you barely have the strength to lift your foot off the ground."

My mother glanced at me and nodded. "You see things in those moments you never expect to see," she said. "A bomb destroying a home, killing the family hiding in their basement. Stepping over body parts as you look for a place to hide your children, knowing no such place exists. It is a life lived in seconds, not years, and you don't come back from that horror the same person you were before."

"The war ended so long ago," one woman said, wiping at her

eyes with a folded handkerchief. "And to me, to us, it feels like it was yesterday."

My mother stood and reached for my hand. "That's because some of us are still at war," she said. "But that war had an end. The one I'm living through now will never end. At least not for me."

MY MOTHER, DESPITE understanding very little English, loved watching television. She had her favorites: *The Honeymooners* because their apartment looked as flimsy as ours; *Combat!* because it was set during World War II; *Divorce Court* for obvious reasons; and *Highway Patrol* because the lead actor, Broderick Crawford, resembled a fruit peddler she knew back in Ischia. But her very favorite performer and the leader of the pack for all the Italian women I knew was Perry Como.

Como was my mother's idea of the perfect man. He was a barber out of Philadelphia who became a successful singer and the darling of middle-aged Italian American women nationwide. My mother and the other women of the neighborhood saw him as the ideal husband, father, provider, a deeply religious man who cared for and nurtured those around him. In other words, he was the exact opposite of the men they shared their unhappy lives with. I never knew if any of what they believed about their favorite singer was true. To them the facts didn't really matter—they believed what they saw on their televisions.

Perry Como had two yearly specials—one to celebrate Christmas, the other Easter—which were required viewing for every member of the family, especially the husbands. It was a scene repeated twice a year in our apartment. My mother, surrounded by a small cluster of Italian women, sitting in one section of the living room, anxiously awaiting the start of the special. The men, my father among them, hunkered down on the other end, dreading the hour they had to endure. During the closing number of both specials, Como would come out, surrounded by a UN contingent of children. This was the golden moment my mother and her friends cherished the most. Their commentary never varied.

"Look how many grandchildren he has," my mother would say, dabbing at her tears as Como prepared to sing the "Ave Maria."

One year I had the temerity to mention that those adoring children surrounding the crooner might actually be actors and not his grandchildren. One of the ladies sitting behind me slapped the back of my head with a rolled-up prayer book. "Why would he need actors when he has all these beautiful grandchildren?" she said.

"I don't know," I said. "But he sure has a lot of them."

"He's been blessed," my mother said. "A good man who leads a good life is always blessed. Especially a man who loves and cares for his wife and his family." She cast an angry gaze toward my father, who simply shrugged and turned back to watch the rest of the program.

"And bad things happen to married men who go around and sleep with tramps," my mother continued. "They will all suffer and know nothing but misery in their lives."

I glanced at my father and could see his body starting to tense. "You don't know anything about him," I said to my mother. "You see him on television and what you see is all you know. And you're seeing exactly what he wants you to see. It's a show. It's not real. None of it."

My mother stared down at me for a few moments and then turned to the other women in the room. "Ignore what he says," she said, pointing to me. "He doesn't know anything. He has never been around a happy marriage. He's never been in the company of a good man. He has no idea what that looks like. And when he grows up, he won't be anything like Perry Como. He'll be exactly like his father.

I pity the woman who will one day end up by his side. Her life will be nothing short of hell. Just like mine."

"Leave him be, Raffaela," one of the women in the room said. "He's only a boy. It's too early to know what he's going to do with his life."

Mrs. Antonelli, a cup of tea cradled in her hands, looked at me and smiled. "My son, Anthony, tells me your boy likes to write stories. He's seen a few and says they're very good. Maybe that's what he'll end up doing."

"Then he *will* be just like his father," my mother said. "Telling stories and taking money from working people who believe what he tells them. That's not a life for any man."

"It doesn't have to be that way," Mrs. Antonelli said. She was a short woman with an easy manner, quick with a smile or a warm embrace. She was about ten years older than my mother and had been through her own share of misery. But any problems that might have existed behind the closed doors of her apartment she kept to herself. "The stories we see every day in the papers, in the magazines, in books, are put in there by people who tell stories. Who says that your boy can't be like one of them?"

My mother looked down at me and shook her head. "That's only a dream, and those don't come true for people like us," she said. "We're caught in the middle of a nightmare, without escape. It's true for me and it's true for him."

My mother then turned her eyes back to the television screen, tears once again streaming down her face, and lost herself in her own dream. She listened to Perry Como sing a string of holiday songs, remembering what it was like when she was a young woman leading a happy life in a place far away.

I never took my mother's negative comments to heart and I never let them deter me from whatever goals I set for myself, either as a boy or when I was old enough to strike out on my own. Not to say her words didn't sting, because they did. No son wants to hear such words from his own mother. But I used them to drive myself forward, and with each passing year my resolve grew to prove her wrong. I was left with no choice but to turn her harmful words into fuel for the fire that guided me even when the path proved daunting.

There was one element of my mother's life that did make me angry and still does to this day, years after her passing: She willingly made herself a victim. That was something I could never understand. She claimed she wanted her freedom, to be able to live her own life and not be dependent on my father for her day-to-day needs. Instead, she did the exact opposite.

She lived in New York for thirty-five years and, other than a handful of words, never bothered to learn the language. There were dozens of Italian-owned shops and stores in the area always in need of extra help, but my mother never once looked for a job, regardless of how desperate we were for money to pay the rent, electric bill, or tuition for her sons. She never left the apartment unless it was to go to the grocery shop or to church. In so many ways, the prison she was confined to was one she herself helped build. She was dependent on my father, and that, more than the violence that always surrounded her, was what made her his captive.

And by extension made me one, as well.

THE NIGHT BEFORE my first trip to Italy, to visit Ischia for the first time, while I was running an errand for my mother, she got into a heated argument with my father. Without having to be told, I knew it was over the usual topic of money gone missing or gambled away, money that was desperately needed to pay our monthly bills. Their argument ended, as they almost always did, with a flurry of powerful blows aimed at her by my father.

By the time I got back to the apartment, my father was gone and my mother was sitting on a dining room chair, a thick cloth filled with ice cubes pressed to her swollen face. Her neck was bruised and red, and her lower lip was tinged with dried blood. I went over to her and removed the cloth filled with ice and saw that there was a thin line of blood coming down from the side of her head.

"We need to go to the hospital," I said to her in a soft voice. "You might need some stitches."

My mother shook her head. "It's not a deep cut," she said. "It will heal by itself in a few days."

"I can't go to Italy," I said to her. "I can't leave you like this."

"There's nothing you can do to stop it," she said. "And you need to go to Ischia. It's important, not just for you but for me."

"Why?"

"I need you to see that not everyone lives like we do," my mother said. "That there are husbands who love their wives and take care of their families. That not everyone is looking to take money that doesn't belong to them. That there are good people who care for each other, who make each other laugh when times are good and are there for one another when tears need to be shed. You need to see that and you need to see it now, while you're still young. Before it's too late."

"If it's as great a place as you say it is," I said, "then why not just go back? Live your life there. Get away from all of this."

"I'm coming over sometime in August," she said. "For a week."

"A week's not good enough," I said. "You should stay there. With your family."

"I can't," my mother said, each word weighed down by the burdens of her sadness and pain. "He'll come after me. Force me to come back with him. It's how he's made. He will find me in Ischia and he will kill me. And if you're with me, he'll come for you, too. There's no escape. Not from him."

"There has to be a way," I said. "Maybe your family can get you a lawyer or go to the police. You have to do something. You can't keep taking these beatings."

"I won't put my family in the middle of this," my mother said. "I don't tell them much about the way we live. I'm embarrassed by it. They work hard and they care for each other. They don't need to know about the debts we have or the beatings we both take. They don't need to know any of that."

"Then it's never going to end," I said. "It's only going to get worse."

She lowered her head and began to cry, the tears running off her face and onto her fingers. "I pray every day," she said between sobs. "To Jesus and all the saints. I pray that they take him. I pray that he will be found dead somewhere. That's the only way for this to end."

I rested an arm around her shoulders and looked out an open window, the curtains moving slightly as a warm breeze came into the apartment. "Nobody's listening, Mom," I said. "Those prayers are a waste of time."

"They are all I have," my mother said. "I have nothing else."

1971 — 1975

❦

ONE MONTH BEFORE my seventeenth birthday, I took the subway to Brooklyn and signed up for a three-year stint in the Navy.

By this time, we were living in the Wakefield section of the East Bronx, in a private home on Boyd Avenue owned by a retired couple, who lived on the top two floors of the house. My father had rented their basement apartment, a place that was barely large enough for one person, let alone three. There was a kitchen, a bedroom, and a living room. I slept on a pullout couch in the living room. The windows opened onto the sidewalk, where we could see the feet of people passing by, walking their dogs or tossing their cigarette butts against the glass. In the years I lived there, we never had company and I never brought any of my high school or work friends to visit. There was only one large pipe, in the middle of a tiny foyer, to warm the apartment in the winter. The bathroom had a shower but no tub. The owners had rented it to my father with the idea that it would be a temporary arrangement, until he could find a more suitable place for his family.

We lived there for six years.

I was attending Mount Saint Michael Academy and working part-time at a dry-cleaning store on East 241st Street, where I was paid off the books. I handed my mother my salary every Saturday and was allowed to keep five dollars for pocket money from the twenty-five I earned. My half brother, after years spent fending for himself, had succeeded in making a life of his own. He was married, had a growing family, and had bought a house on Ely Avenue, a ten-minute walk from our tiny little apartment.

I admired him from a distance, proud to see he hadn't let my father's cruelty prevent him from finding his place in the world. When I was young, he worked at a series of banks and attended college at night. He became a CPA and by the time he had moved into his new home in the Bronx was a middle-management executive at American Express. My half brother kept his head down and focused on the road in front of him. I cannot say he and I are close, even to this day. The age difference is one factor. Our different personalities another. My mother's open display of affection toward him and casual indifference to me perhaps a third. But I grew to respect him. He asked nothing from anyone, and whatever he has achieved in life has been the benefit of his own hard work.

I did wonder, however, during those difficult early years, why he never made an effort to get our mother away from my father. I felt back then that he was the only one with a shot at convincing her to pack her bags and return to Ischia. I admit I was troubled for a number of years at what seemed to me like his indifference to our mother's plight.

Looking back now, with some years behind me, I can find no fault with his inaction. He was, at the time, doing all he could to simply survive. As a young man he found himself in a strange country, having to quickly learn a new language and adapt to a new way of life. There were months, sometimes years, when I didn't know where he was living, with whom, or how exactly he was surviving. He was, for the most part, alone. And yet, through hard work and sheer determination, he found his way. He clearly knew the physical and financial issues our mother was forced to deal with, and it must have cost him many a sleepless night and much consternation. Perhaps making his own way against the odds, making a life for himself, was its own victory.

In truth, there was nothing for any of us to do—not me, not our family in Italy, not my half brother. The only one who could have broken us away from my father's hold was my mother, and she chose not to take that path for reasons of her own.

By the time I was seventeen, I had reached a point of desperation. I was living with my parents in a dank basement apartment under the dark clouds of debt and violence and found my day-to-day existence under those conditions unsustainable. The Navy offered me a way out.

They offered a decent salary, an opportunity to continue my education free of charge, and also promised to honor my request that my three-year stint would be based in Naples, Italy. That would place me a mere eighteen miles from Ischia, which at this time in my life I had embraced as my true home. I filled out the forms I was given, spoke at length to a recruiting officer, and was told I would begin my naval career as an E-3 unless I changed my mind in the next forty-eight hours.

My subway ride back to the Bronx from Brooklyn was a happy one. I had the promise of a new future ahead of me, a future spent far away from my parents, one that would allow me to forge my own path in life. I would still be able to send money back home and even had a semblance of hope that with me stationed in Naples, my mother might find the strength to finally leave my father and head back to Ischia.

It was a teenager's dream, one that would not come true.

I came home from the recruiter and found my mother in her usual place—sitting on a kitchen chair, listening to an Italian radio station. I turned off the radio, pulled back a chair, and sat down across from her. I told her that I had signed up for a three-year period of service. I told her I would be stationed in Naples and had filled out a form to have a large chunk of my monthly salary sent to her.

My mother sat there and listened, her hands trembling, her eyes wide with a combination of fear and horror. She didn't speak, and her face and neck were coated with thin lines of sweat.

I reached out a hand to grasp one of hers, and my mother pulled back. She stood up so suddenly that she toppled her chair. She turned, opened a cabinet door, and pulled out a large kitchen carving knife. She stared at me, her entire body trembling, and held the sharp end of the knife to her throat. "I will kill myself if you do this," she shouted. "I'll do it right here, right in front of you. My blood, my death, will be on your hands."

I stood and moved a few inches closer to my mother. "Mom, calm down," I said. "Put down that knife, sit down, and we can talk."

"If you leave me with him, I will be found dead," she said. "So why not let me die now? In front of you? I'll let you be the one to tell him. He killed one wife on his own. Now, today, you can help him kill a second one."

"Please, please put down the knife," I said. "I have forty-eight hours to change my mind. I don't have to leave."

"Everything I've had to live through—the beatings, the trips to the hospital, the debts, staying in an apartment the size of a prison cell—has all been because of you. If you weren't born, I would be home now. But because you lived, I stayed and I suffered. And now you want to be the one to leave. To escape from him, to escape from all this misery. You can escape if you want. But first you have to stand there and watch me die."

I stared at my mother and shook my head. "You don't have to kill yourself," I said. "I'm going to call the guy at the Navy and tell him

I changed my mind. I'm not going to join the Navy. I'm going to stay here. With you and with him."

"Don't lie to me," my mother shouted. "I'm married to a liar. One is enough. I don't need another one."

"I'm not lying to you," I said. "I'm going to the other room and make the call. If you decide to kill yourself while I'm on the phone, it won't be because I joined the Navy. It will be because I decided to stay with you."

My mother moved the knife away from her throat, and I lowered my head and turned to walk out of the kitchen. Then, speaking in a lower and much calmer voice, she said, "You need to find a second job. The rent is due in two weeks, and I only have half of it. And it doesn't look like I'm going to be getting any money from your father."

I turned back, looked at her, nodded, then walked out of the kitchen and into the tiny living room. I sat on the couch and reached for the phone. For a few minutes I quietly looked down at the signed Navy documents in my hands. I dialed the number of the Navy recruiter and in a few brief minutes brought an end to what only hours earlier had felt like my escape route.

I hung up the phone, weighed down with a sadness I had never felt before, and wondered if I would ever be free.

I HAD FINISHED high school and was about to begin my first full-time job, working in the check-reconcilement department at Manufacturers Hanover Trust Bank on Water Street at a weekly salary of ninety-five dollars. I was happy to have landed the position, especially when I learned that the bank would pay for any college business courses I chose to take. And my mother was even happier, thrilled that I would be making steady take-home money.

The day I told her I had been hired, she looked at me, pressed both hands against my arms, and said, "Do everything they ask you to do. This is a good job at a good place. Don't lose it. And don't ever leave. You will never find something this good again."

I pulled away from her and shook my head. "I'm not looking to make a career out of this," I said. "I'll learn as much as I can from it, take as many night classes as I can, and then I'll move on."

"To what?" my mother asked. "What will you find that's going to be better than what you've already found?"

"I would love to get a job on a newspaper," I said. "It's what I've always wanted to do. I mean, I don't know if I can make that happen. But I need to at least give it a try."

"Becoming a writer is just a dream you have," my mother said. "It's not possible, not for people like us. Do you know anyone who makes their living doing that? You read all these books, newspapers, magazines. Do you know anyone who does what you dream of doing?"

"No," I said.

"You were lucky you found this job at the bank," she said. "That's a real job with real money paid to you every week. This idea you have about becoming a writer is the talk of a boy. You're past that now. Put away the dream."

"Maybe you're right," I said. "Maybe it's not meant to be, not for me, anyway. But I'm still going to give it a try."

"You'll be wasting your time," my mother said. "And throwing away a good job with a future. You'll be just like your father, moving from job to job with nothing to show for it. Get this writing business out of your head. It's not for you."

"You don't know anything about it," I said. "The more you tell me not to do it, the more I want to prove to you I can."

"Just to prove me wrong?"

"No," I said. "Just to prove me right. It's true, I don't know anybody who writes books or works on a newspaper or a magazine. That makes it harder for me to get in the door. But that doesn't mean I'll quit trying."

My mother moved away from me and sat down, wiping at her lips with a folded handkerchief. She stayed quiet for several moments, gazing out a small window to the street outside. "What will you write about?" she finally asked. "What stories will you tell?"

"I'm not sure," I said. "I've written a few down, but I don't know how good they are."

"I used to like to tell stories," my mother said. "Many years ago, when I was much younger. I would tell them to my little brothers when they were getting ready for bed."

"What kind of stories?" I asked.

"They liked ones that made them stay up later than they should, talking to one another in the dark," my mother said. "Stories about demons and ghosts and witches."

"Scary stories," I said, smiling at her. "Perfect for bedtime."

"I told them one about a Nazi soldier walking in a heavy rain late at night on the streets of Ischia," my mother said. She sat up in her chair, her eyes animated, her hands resting gently on the top of the kitchen table. "This soldier had done some horrible things to so many people during the war. Tortured children, shot and killed old people, raped wives in front of their husbands."

"This is what you told three little boys before they were supposed to go to sleep?" I asked. "The 'Three Little Pigs' story would have worked and maybe not have given them nightmares."

"I don't know that story," my mother said. "And a story—a good story—is one that isn't a fairy tale. It's one that shows you the world and how it really is."

"Go on," I said. "I can't wait to hear how it ends."

"The soldier stops in front of Saint Peter's Church," my mother said. "He is desperate to get out of the pouring rain and get dry and spend a few minutes in a quiet place. He opens the door and goes inside. The church is empty. The only light is from the votive candles in front of the saints and on the altar. He walks to the front pew and sits there."

"This is not going to have a happy ending, is it?" I said.

"I don't know any stories with happy endings," my mother said. "Anyway, the soldier sits for the longest time, his drenched clothes dripping water onto the ground. He leans his head back and closes his eyes. And then he hears the screams and the cries and the moans of all those he tormented. He sits up, opens his eyes, and looks around the empty church. No one is there, but the noise only grows louder, and then he begins to see the faces of all those he harmed."

"Your brothers must have been scared out of their heads," I said.

"They held on to each other and didn't dare move their eyes from me," my mother said, smiling.

"So, what happens next?"

"The soldier stands up to leave the pew and run out of the church," my mother said. "But before he can move, the floor from the center of the altar slides open. Flames shoot out from under the church. Smoke rises and a figure stands before him, looking at the soldier, laughing at him. The figure points to the soldier and then looks down to the flames below. 'You belong to me now,' the figure tells the soldier. 'You will now suffer as you have made others suffer, tonight and for all of eternity.' With that, the figure reaches for the soldier, who still stands there, frozen in place. The figure grabs the soldier by his uniform collar and tosses him down into the fiery pit. He then follows the soldier down. The floor gently closes. No more flames, no more smoke, no more cries or moans. The church is empty once again. The only sound you hear is of the falling rain outside."

I stared at my mother. "I'm really glad you never told me a bedtime story," I said.

"Did you like it?"

"I did," I said. "Very much."

"Maybe one day, if you have children of your own, you can share it with them," she said. "They don't need to know it's from me. Tell them it's your story. They'll appreciate it more."

I SAT NEXT to my mother in the center pew of our local church. She was clutching rosary beads in her hands and mumbling a prayer. My mother attended the 9 A.M. mass most mornings and would, on occasion, ask me to accompany her. Like many religious Italian mothers, she had a dream that I would enter the priesthood, a dream I dashed early on, despite the two years of hope my time as an altar boy gave her.

"We get the new priest today," I said to her. "They always break in the new priests with the weekday masses."

My mother shrugged. "New, old, doesn't matter to me," she said. "Since they switched the mass to English, I don't know what they're saying anyway."

"Did you do this when you were in Italy?" I asked. "Go to mass every day?"

"No," my mother said. "Just on Sundays. But I had less to pray for in those years."

"I like church when it's empty," I said. "When I have it all to myself and can pray if I want or just sit and get away from my life for a few quiet minutes."

"You'll be away from all of this soon enough," my mother said.

"You just need to hang on for a few more years. And then you'll have your freedom. A job, a wife, maybe even a couple of children of your own."

I looked at my mother and shook my head. "I have no plans to get married," I said. "I've spent too many years watching you and my father fighting. And even when you're not arguing, there's a constant fear—of the phone ringing and the voice at the other end asking for money or a knock on the door and a loan shark looking for cash that should have been handed over weeks ago. I don't want any part of that."

"You'll change your mind," my mother said. "And it won't be the same for you as it is for me. The orphan will prevent all that."

"What orphan?" I asked, my voice a bit louder than I had intended.

My mother smiled and rested her rosary beads on her lap. "You know I send a little bit of money each month to the girls' orphanage in Pompeii," she said. "To the nuns there."

"Two dollars every month," I said. "Like clockwork."

"I wish I could send more," she said. "They do God's work. A few years ago, I wrote and asked the Mother Superior to help find a bride for you. They raise the orphans until they're eighteen years old. Last year I got a letter back telling me they found someone who they think would make a great wife for you. A young girl who has always wanted to come live in America."

I was stunned for a few moments. I knew my mother wasn't joking—she seldom did and never about religious matters. But she couldn't possibly be serious about an arranged marriage between me and an orphan girl I had never met. "Why would you even think of something like that?" was all I could manage to say.

"It's a perfect situation," my mother said. "You know all the

problems your father's family caused me, all the money, aggrava-
tion, and arguments. You'll be free of that married to an orphan. It
will just be the two of you. And you can build a life together."

"Your marriage was arranged," I said. "How has that turned out?"

"That was a mistake," my mother said. "And I didn't marry an
orphan. I married a murderer."

"I'm not marrying anybody," I said. "Especially an orphan from
Pompeii."

"She's smart, speaks English, and is very pretty," my mother
said. "They say she knows how to cook, but what she doesn't know
I can teach her."

"So, she's not really a wife for me," I said. "More like a friend for
you."

My mother patted my right knee and nodded. "When you're
ready, you let me know," she said. "I'll take care of the rest. And
whatever you do, don't mention a word of this to your father."

"Don't worry," I said, sliding out of the pew. "I'll never mention
a word of this to *anyone*."

My mother would continue to mention the orphan periodically
over the next few years. I never took the notion seriously. Instead, I
would smile and tell her, "When I'm ready to get married, you'll be
the first to know. And she better be as pretty as you say she is."

"Even prettier," my mother would say, always with a smile. "The
two of you will be so happy together. It will be a marriage made in
heaven. Not like mine. My marriage was made in hell."

I HAD ENROLLED at St. John's University in Queens and signed up
to take two classes for six credits, two nights a week. I took out a
$1,500 loan from a Bronx bank to buy a used Toyota Corolla, and I
would drive into the city on the nights I had classes, leaving right

after work. Taking six credits a semester would, I calculated, earn me a college degree in just under twelve years. Still, it was a start.

It had been a cold winter's day, and I dreaded the walk from the bank office to my parked car and the long drive out to Jamaica for ninety minutes of a tedious marketing class. I had just put on my coat and was about to reach for my shoulder bag when the phone on my desk rang. I picked it up on the third ring and listened for several moments. On the other end was the calm, soothing voice of a doctor working in the emergency room at Misericordia Hospital, which was less than a ten-minute walk from my parents' apartment.

He told me my mother was brought into the emergency room by a friend. My mother was bleeding from a wound on the back of her head and had bruises on her arms, legs, and neck. She also had severe abdominal pain, probably caused by blunt force. He needed to run some tests and she was being admitted. He told me to come as soon as I could but not to rush since she most likely would be there for several days.

"Can she talk?" I asked.

"Her English isn't very good," the doctor said. "And I'm afraid my Italian is even worse. But, yes, she can talk. She gave me this number to call you."

"Thanks, Doctor," I said. "I'll be there soon as I can. Less than an hour."

"She should be in a room by the time you get here," the doctor said. "The nurse at the front desk will give you the room number."

I got in my car and drove back up to the East Bronx. This was not the first time I had to visit my mother in a hospital room, and I never had to work too hard to figure out who it was that had put her there. Over the years, my father's hands had done a great deal of damage, to my mother and to me. By the time I was nine, I had had more stitches sewn on my body than I could count. And one time I needed to be kept at Saint Clare's Hospital overnight due to a concussion, caused by being thrown against the edge of a radiator. Those were minor incidents compared to what my mother had endured.

My father was usually careful not to hit her in the face, so he had to have lost all control over his temper when he administered this latest beating. Most of his blows usually landed on her back, legs, and in the center of her stomach. Once he punched himself out to the point of exhaustion, my father would leave the apartment and disappear for several days. When he returned, he came seeking forgiveness, often with tears in his eyes, repeating over and over how sorry he was for the damage he had caused.

My mother was in a small room with two beds. She was in the one closest to the curtained window. The first bed was occupied by an elderly Hispanic woman who was sound asleep, oxygen tubes inserted in her nose and an IV drip attached to one of her arms. A thin curtain separated the two beds.

I walked over to my mother's bed. She was sitting up, staring out the closed window at the buildings across the way. There was a small bandage on her right cheek, and both eyes were red, puffy, and bruised. "Don't tell anyone I'm here," she said. "I don't want anyone to know."

I looked at the marks on her arms and saw the IV needle sending fluids into her right arm. "What started it this time?" I asked.

She shrugged. "What always starts it," my mother said. "Money. The money we don't have. The money he gambles away. The money he spends on strangers and his family. The money we need to pay our bills. The money we need to live."

"Does he know you're in the hospital?"

"He threw me against the refrigerator and then walked out of the apartment," she said. "He slammed the door shut behind him. He'll be gone for a few days. But he'll be back. That's the one thing you can always count on him to do—he comes back."

"I haven't had a chance to talk to the doctor yet," I said. "So I don't know how long you'll be in here or how serious your injuries are. The doctor probably won't be back around until the morning. He'll have the test results by then."

"They brought me down and took some pictures of my stomach," she said. "Put me behind a machine. And they took some blood."

I looked up at the television bolted to the wall. "Is there anything you want to watch?" I said. "Or would you rather get some sleep?"

She shrugged again. "If there's wrestling on, I'll watch. If not, don't bother. I'm too tired to look at anything I won't be able to understand."

I reached up to turn on the television and smiled. "In that case, let's see if we can find ourselves a few wrestling bouts."

My mother loved wrestling and, like many of the other Italian women in both the Little Naples and Hell's Kitchen neighborhoods we had lived in, followed it with a fan's fervor. She would also argue with you passionately if you even hinted that the matches were staged.

When we lived in Hell's Kitchen, Madison Square Garden was on 50th Street and Eighth Avenue and hosted wrestling matches once a month. For six dollars, my mother, along with many women from the neighborhood, would go see the matches and make a night of it. As I got older, I grew to think of it as live theater for the poor. It was three hours of pure entertainment, and they loved every minute of it. Those were the years when the wrestling champion was one of their own—Bruno Sammartino, an Italian. And the villains were men they could vilify and boo—from Gorilla Monsoon to Killer Kowalski to the Von Erich brothers.

My mother would often take me with her on those Monday nights out. It was one of the few passions she shared with my father, and they both believed there were many life lessons to be learned from watching a night of professional wrestling.

"You remember those nights when we went to the Garden to see them wrestle in person?" I asked her.

My mother nodded and smiled. "Every match," she said. "My favorite was when Sammartino lifted that giant of a man on his back. What was his name?"

"Haystacks Calhoun," I said.

"They said he weighed six hundred pounds," my mother said. "I still don't know how Bruno got him on his back."

"I'm pretty sure they worked it out in advance," I said.

"I know you think I was foolish to believe it was real," she said. "But there's a lot to be learned from wrestling. Every bout tells you a story. You have the good guys and you have your bad. But sometimes the ones you think are good turn around and betray you. And the ones you always thought were bad turn out to have a good side. And then there are those who never change at all. It's a lot like life."

"Maybe," I said. "But in life—real life, anyway—the story isn't written out for us. We have no idea how it's going to turn out. We don't know which good guy is going to turn against us and which bad guy is going to come to our rescue."

"But we do know the ones who will always be bad," my mother said. "Men like your father. They were born bad and there's nothing you can do to change them. That part always stays the same, no matter what story you decide to tell."

I looked at her and rested a hand on top of hers. "Maybe you're the one that should be the writer," I said. "Instead of me."

"We both know how my story is going to end," my mother said. "I don't need to write it down. Living it is bad enough."

I sat on a torn leather chair close to her bed, my hand still on top of hers, her wrist bandaged and blotches of dry blood seeping through. "The bad guy doesn't always win, Mom," I said. "Most of the time, he's the one that loses in the end."

My mother reached up her hand and rubbed her fingers against a side of my face. "Maybe in your stories that might be true," she said. "But not in mine."

1976-1988

✧

I WAS NOT, thankfully, destined to have a career in banking. Instead, I was determined to get a job at a newspaper, despite what my mother had said. I applied for a job as a copy boy at the New York *Daily News* and quickly received a rejection letter. By this time I had started writing for a couple of small newspapers to at least have some clips to send along with my meager résumé. One of the papers was *The Torch*, a weekly put out by St. John's University. The features editor there told me the best way to get a job was to have someone working at the paper use their name on the application as a recommended hire. I didn't know anyone who worked there. But, luckily, the film critic of the paper, Kathleen Carroll, taught a class at St. John's. The features editor told me to get a new application and assigned me to write a profile about Kathleen and the work she did. A few days later, I was sitting across from her in the features department of the *Daily News*.

It was my first time visiting a newspaper office, and I fought to contain my excitement. During the course of the interview, Kathleen asked what kind of work I was interested in. I told her I wanted to work at the paper and had an application with me. Kathleen then uttered the words I desperately needed to hear. She said, "If there's anything I can do to help, let me know." I pulled the application out of my bag and asked if she would sign the back and allow me to use her as a reference. She took the application, flipped it over, and signed her name. "I doubt it will do you much good," she said. "But good luck."

A week later, I was summoned to the office of Ed Quinn, the personnel director of the paper, and was offered a copy boy's position, making $134 a week, based solely on the fact that Kathleen Carroll was gracious enough to vouch for me despite not knowing me very well. I owe the start of my career to her, and I cannot ever thank her enough.

My mother opposed the move at first, concerned that the newspaper job wouldn't last, while banks were always open for business. But the boost in income from $95 to $134 a week quelled some of her fears. Plus, it was a union job, which in her mind meant I could never be fired, no matter how incompetent I was. It also allowed us to move into a larger one-bedroom apartment, on East 234th Street off White Plains Road.

My father was opposed to the move since the monthly rent was higher than that for the basement apartment, which he had grown fond of. For years I wondered why he felt so comfortable living in such tight quarters, until my mother explained it to me. "Your father spent nearly eight years in a prison cell, no bigger than a closet," she said. "Not only was he used to living in a small space, he found comfort in it. To him, that tiny apartment must have felt like a mansion."

My father continued his scamming ways, and the physical side of his nature had not tempered with age. He would work for a few weeks, having long ago given up his job at the meat market. Instead, he was earning pocket money at a shoeshine parlor on the West Side of Manhattan. On a good day, he would earn as much as forty dollars, half of which always was spent on racehorses.

While most of my friends—old ones from the bank and new ones from the paper—were moving on from their family homes to live in apartments of their own, I didn't dare contemplate such a move. To begin with, I was paying if not all of the rent then certainly the bulk of it. On top of which there were monthly expenses. But, more important, I needed my father to know I was still around. I lived with the quiet but nagging fear that my father would one day snap and end my mother's life, the same way he had ended his first wife's after only six years of marriage.

We didn't socialize much in those days. By this point, my mother seemed to close herself off even more than before, her days spent in prayer or sitting in the kitchen, seething with pent-up anger. Despite my many pleas for her to pack up and go to Ischia, she refused to move.

"So long as your father takes a breath, he will be a danger to me and to you," she said to me one afternoon, bruises visible on her lower legs and upper arms. "He doesn't know how to live in peace. He knows only how to create problems, and then he tosses those problems to us. For us to fix. It's a cycle without end."

"I wish I knew what he did with all the money he scams from people," I said. "It's not a couple of hundred dollars. He takes people for thousands with his cons, but he never has anything left after it's all said and done. Does he just gamble it all away?"

"A lot of it goes to that," my mother said. "Some more is given to his family. And I suspect he even finds a way to use some of it to buy whatever his daughter might need."

I turned to face my mother, unable to hide the surprised look on my face. "His daughter?" I said. "What the hell do you mean, his daughter? He never said anything to me about a daughter."

My mother nodded. "There's a lot of things you weren't supposed to know," she said. "Secrets his family kept from you. The murder was one. His daughter was another."

"Why didn't you tell me?" I asked.

"I'm telling you now," she said. "It wouldn't have done any good to tell you when you were a boy. What were you going to do, run out and look for her? Your father isn't allowed to see her, at least that's what I was told. She was six when he killed her mother and she was taken away from his family and raised by an aunt—one of her mother's sisters, I think."

"How do you know he sees her now?" I asked.

"The murder happened a long time ago," my mother said. "They didn't check on your father when he was first let out of prison, so I doubt they're keeping an eye on him now. And I've looked at the bills over the years. There was one from Macy's for a washing machine and a dryer. Look around. You see either of those in this kitchen? And there were others along the same lines."

"Do you have any idea where she is?" I asked. "Where she lives?"

She shook her head. "I've heard she lives in Brooklyn, is married, has children," she said. "But that's all secondhand. It might be true or it might be just another story."

"Have you ever met her?"

"No," my mother said. "But you have. Years ago, at a family party. You weren't told she was your sister. I don't remember now who they told you she was—a family friend, maybe. You told me about her when you came home that night. You were about ten years old. You told me you were in the back seat of a car being driven home and there was this very nice girl sitting next to you. She said you were a nice boy and she was glad she had the chance to meet you. Do you remember any of that?"

I looked at my mother and stayed silent for several moments. "I do," I said. "I remember she had dark curly hair and a nice smile. It was tight in the back seat of the car, and we were all crunched in together. She talked to me for the whole trip. They let her out first. I don't remember where. But I do remember she told me she hoped we would see each other again."

"She lost her mother in the worst way I could imagine," she said. "She's suffered more than enough in this lifetime."

"Why would she want to see him?" I asked.

"I'm not the one to ask," my mother said. "I'm the one who married the man who killed his wife."

I left the apartment and went out for a long walk, with no particular destination in mind. It was closing in on winter and the air was cold, and my leather jacket did little to ward off the winds whipping down the side streets of the East Bronx. But I didn't notice. I just kept walking, head down, hands jammed inside the front pockets of my blue jeans. I had a sister. And she lived somewhere in New York City, and I knew then what I still know today, all these decades later. The two of us would never meet again. That connection to her was denied me by my father's crime.

I had been angry at my father ever since I found out about the murder, but now my hatred reached an even deeper level. He was a man who acted without thought, who didn't care enough about a little girl, his own daughter, to spare her mother's life. The jealous rage that had consumed him allowed no room for him to care for the child he was about to leave behind. I can't imagine what her life must have been like, knowing how her mother died, knowing that the man who killed her now tried to make amends by doling out cash or appliances. I'll never know, because he also ripped from me any chance of knowing my sister.

It is an odd feeling to not know where or how she is, and it troubles me to this day. I have no idea if she's alive, no notion of the kind of life she led, if she had made her peace with my father or even grew to forgive him for what he had done. She was a stranger to me then and remains a mystery to me now.

I met her once, sitting in the back seat of a car. Her face, her smile, her words, forever etched in my mind.

They are all I have of my sister. And all I will ever have.

WORKING AS A copy boy was not quite what I expected it to be. I spent nine miserable months driving drunk editors home to Westchester in battered *Daily News* cars, making coffee and lunch runs, returning dresses from the women's department, and sitting in a dimly lit closet sharpening boxes of pencils. It was a worthless, thankless job, but it did serve two purposes: It got me into a room at what was, at the time, the largest circulation daily in America, and I got to spend time with the two columnists who would prove to be guiding lights in my still-to-be-born career—Pete Hamill and Jimmy Breslin.

I had started freelancing for two new monthly publications and, thanks to an introduction from Hamill, the *SoHo Weekly News,* which was then a competitor to *The Village Voice.* The editor there, Al Ellenberg, gave me the run of the city and allowed me to pitch my own ideas. Assuming they passed his editorial smell test, he printed them. In return, I was paid five dollars per article. I even managed to get a few pieces into the *Daily News,* for free. But I wasn't looking for money. I was looking for clips to show editors, with the idea that those published articles would lead to more assignments. Plus, I took some sound advice from Jimmy Breslin: "When you're starting out, never look at what it pays," he told me one day as I was waiting for him to finish one of his columns. "You need to pile up the clips. But if you turn out to be any good and you make it in this business, then you don't even write out a Christmas card for less than ten thousand dollars."

I was in awe of their talents, and they both will always have a special place in my heart. I would put copies of every article I had published on their desks and hope they would give them a look and offer feedback. They did more than that, much more. Hamill sat with me and broke down my story sentence by sentence, guiding me, a master taking a student under his wing. Breslin, as was his way, did not say anything until the articles piled up on a side of his desk. I figured he was too busy to read them and was about to give up any hope of getting feedback. Then, one late afternoon, we happened to be standing next to each other in a crowded elevator. "You're ending too many of your sentences in '-ing' words," he said to me. "Those are weak. You need more words ending in '-ed.' Those are stronger. Think of it like a musician. He always finishes his piece strong. Other than that, keep it up."

At the end of my nine months as a copy boy, I was promoted to yet another thankless job. But at least this one came with a desk and a chair and, more important, a $100 raise, pushing my salary up to $234 a week. I was promoted to movie-timetable clerk, which meant typing more than twenty pages a day of movie listings and showtimes for the theaters in the five boroughs. My desk mate took care of Westchester, Suffolk, and Nassau counties. Across from me sat the three who were tasked with the television listings—another mind-numbing chore.

Despite the drudgery of the work, I began to feel as if I was at least making some progress. My mother was pleased with the increase in salary and was even more impressed when I showed her the first check I ever received for writing a magazine article. It was for a new Italian American publication called *Identity*. In return for writing 1,200 words about the horn many young Italian American men wore around their necks, I was paid $150. My mother held that check in her hand and stared at it for several moments. Then she rested it on her lap and looked up at me, tears welling in her eyes. "They paid you to tell them a story," she managed to say. "I never believed something like this would happen. I never thought people got paid to tell stories. I never believed you. I'm sorry. I just didn't know."

"Let's not get crazy," I said, trying to lighten her mood. "It's a new magazine, and it's easier for somebody like me to get a shot with them. I can't get into the more popular magazines. So I start with magazines like this and for that paper that pays me five dollars every week for a story."

"Don't show this to your father," she said. "You can show him the story if you want. But don't tell him how much they paid you. It will only lead to trouble."

"He's been in a better mood these last few months," I said. "Maybe the worst is over. He's not a young guy anymore. Maybe he's finally calming down."

My mother shook her head. "Men like your father don't change with age," she said. "They get worse. It's when he's quiet you really need to worry. He's not a man who can be at peace."

"This magazine asked me for another story," I said, eager to ease the conversation away from my father. "I told them I'd give them a few ideas next week."

"Why don't you write one about Padre Pio?" my mother said. "Do you know about him?"

"Is that the guy who bleeds from his hands whenever he serves mass?" I said. "All I know about him is that for some reason his framed photo used to hang in all the shops in Hell's Kitchen. I never could understand why."

"He bleeds from the wounds of Christ during mass," my mother said. "The hands, the front of the feet, and from the side of the ribs. His hands are wrapped in cloth, and you can see the blood seep through."

"And you believe this?" I said.

"I believe it because it's true," my mother said. "He will be a saint one day. He's performed miracles."

"What kind of miracles?"

"I heard of one a few years ago," my mother said. "There was a man who had suffered a horrible accident when he was younger. It cost him his sight and his sense of smell. One day, he waited outside the church where Padre Pio was serving mass. As Padre Pio passed the man, he reached out and handed him a rose. The man put the rose to his nose and for the first time in years was able to smell the flower. That's a miracle."

"It would have been better if Padre Pio had given the guy his eyesight back," I said. "It's a lot better to see than to smell, I would think."

"The man fell to his knees, clutching the rose to his chest," my mother said. "And he was embraced by those around him. They had all been witness to a miracle."

"So, he bleeds from his palms, the tops of his feet, and one side of his rib cage every time he's on the altar," I said. "When does the bleeding start and when does it stop?"

"Why are you asking so many questions?" my mother said. "You either believe or you don't."

"Why do you believe it?"

"Because I know in my heart it's true," my mother said. "There are many men in this world who do horrible things each and every day. They rip you apart and make it so easy to spend your time hating them and the world around you. And then there are the rare good ones. They are the ones that give you hope and a reason to keep living. Padre Pio is one of those men. And that is why I believe. Because I need to."

"It could be a good story," I said to her, smiling. "A priest who bleeds all over the altar at every mass. I might be able to sell the magazine editor on that."

My mother folded the check and stuck it in the front pocket of her housedress. She stood and walked over to me and smiled. "If he does say yes," she said, "what do I get for giving you the story?"

"How about we do this," I said. "I write it and get the credit, and when I get paid you get the check. Even Padre Pio would call that a fair deal."

I was happy to see my mother with a smile on her face. Even more because of what had caused her happiness—my getting paid for writing a story. I realized as I got older that the reasons she had her doubts about my making a career as a writer were not based in hatred or a lack of confidence in my abilities. She simply didn't know that such a career was possible. And to be honest, I wasn't all that sure myself.

But seeing the look in her eyes as she held the magazine open on her lap and stared down at the article I had written was all the proof I needed that I had her blessing to continue. Neither one of us knew what the future would bring, but for now at least we allowed ourselves to enjoy the moment together.

THE FEW HAPPY times I shared with my mother were overwhelmed by the darkness that always surrounded us. At that point in my career, it had been a few months since my father attempted any scams and he had even managed to keep his violent outbursts under control. It was an uneasy peace to be sure, but one I could learn to live with. I was slowly making inroads at the paper, writing a few articles that caught the eye of several of the top editors. I began to think that there was a possibility that I could make a go of the career I very much wanted. My mother no longer disparaged my dream and, in fact, began to encourage it.

The focus on my job and on writing articles caused me to let my guard down. I used to follow my father's mood swings, almost able to predict when the next dark storm would land. But now my time was directed elsewhere, and my father took full advantage.

He had worked his greatest con yet, one that would bring my mother to the brink of a breakdown and lead to our biggest argument to date.

My mother seldom called me at the paper, mostly out of fear that someone else would answer the phone and she would be unable to relay a message without speaking English. I picked up on the second ring. Her voice was shrill and filled with fear, rage, venom. She screamed into the phone, the words loud, shouted out due to resentment and frustration and aimed at the one person she could direct such words to—me.

"They came to the door" were her first words. "Seven of them. They came to the door and forced their way in."

"Who did?" I asked.

"Seven men," she shouted. "I don't know any of them. They said they were related to your father. But I've never seen them before."

"Did they hurt you?"

"I wish that was why they had come," my mother said. "I've grown used to getting beaten. But what they wanted was much worse than a slap or a punch."

"Calm down," I said. "Calm down and tell me what happened."

"What do you think happened?" my mother said, her voice loud enough to be heard by others sitting around my desk, none of whom spoke Italian. "They want their money back. Money your father took from them. They said we had three weeks to pay them. Three weeks."

I closed my eyes and took a deep breath. My neck was damp with sweat, and I couldn't contain the helpless feeling that was slowly surging through my body. "How much does he owe?" I asked.

"Seventeen thousand seven hundred dollars," my mother said.

"And they want it all in three weeks. That's all the time they gave you. Three weeks."

"Gave *me*?" I said, not bothering to hide the surprise in my voice. "I make two hundred thirty-four dollars a week. I have a little over two hundred dollars in my bank account. They can give me three years instead of three weeks and I still won't be able to pay that kind of money back."

"They will kill him if you don't pay them the money," my mother said, her voice softening. "And then they might kill you. I don't know these men, so I don't know what they will do unless they get their money. You have three weeks. You need to figure out a way to pay them."

Then she hung up the phone.

The train ride to the Bronx seemed to last an eternity. Up to this point, I had always managed to bail my father out. It had taken months sometimes and one time even a full year, but I had always paid his debts. But those debts were in the hundreds of dollars, with two or three crossing into the low thousands. It was a drain on my finances and forced me on many occasions to take on more than one job, but I was always able to contain the damage.

This was different. This was a heavyweight debt owed to seven men whose identity I didn't know. I figured them to be working men, my father's most dependable targets, and I also knew they were unlikely to be law-abiding citizens. Every scam my father pulled involved breaking one law or another, and this one, this massive bill tossed onto my lap, would be no different. I also knew my father would be in hiding and would stay hidden until a solution was found. I was never certain where he went during these times of crisis, but I did know that if I ever saw him again it would be after the debt was cleared.

I walked into the apartment and found my mother sitting at the kitchen table, rosary beads in her hands, a small lamp the only light in the room. "I'm praying to Saint Anthony," she said. "Maybe he'll help you find a way to get the money."

"Good idea," I said. "That always works."

She looked up, her face flushed red with anger and her eyes locked on mine, glaring at me in a way she had never done before. "You have to get the money," she said, through gritted teeth. "I'm not touching what I have in Italy. Not for this. Not for your father and not for you."

"Touching what in Italy?" I asked.

"The money I have there," she said. "He doesn't get any of it and neither do you."

I was so stunned I couldn't say a word for several moments. All I could do was look at my mother. "You have money in Italy?" I asked.

She didn't say a word. She only nodded her head slowly.

"You have *this* kind of money?" I asked. "All these years, we're living in one dump after another, I'm working one, sometimes two jobs to help pay the rent and the other bills. To pay off his debts. And all this time, you have money, real money, put away in Italy?"

"The money is not for you," my mother said. "Or for your father. The money is for my son."

I pounded a closed fist on top of the kitchen table, knocking over a religious statue. "*I'm* your son," I said. "I'm the one that's here with you. I'm the one you turn to for money. Me."

"You didn't lose a father the way he did," my mother said. "You weren't kicked out of our home the way he was, forced to live on his own. You didn't have to leave a place where you had family and people that loved you to come to a place that turned its back to you. He had to do all that. He had to find his own way."

"We all had to find our own way," I said.

"You had a home and you had a father," my mother said. "And he was a man you loved more than you loved me, until I told you about what he had done to his first wife. But still, in spite of all the horrible things he did, he loved you. And still does. My son lost that when his father died. And that kind of loss can never be replaced. And that's why whatever I have in Italy belongs to him."

"How much money do you have in Italy?" I asked. "And how did you get it? It can't all be from renting out the two apartments Nonna left you. You don't charge that much, and you're always complaining about the money that's needed to keep up the apartments. So it has to be coming from someplace else."

"Where it comes from is my business," my mother said. "And so is where the money goes."

"Does he know about it?" I asked. "About the money?"

My mother shook her head. "Who?" she said. "Your father? Never. The money would be gone in a matter of months."

"Not my father," I said. "Your son. Does he know about the money?"

"I keep no secrets from him," my mother said. "Besides, he works in a bank. With important people. He understands about money. Not like you. All you care about are stories you want to tell, and then you have to hope people like them enough to pay you."

I stayed silent for several moments. My mother sat inches from me, her face red and her hands trembling. "Did you get their names?" I asked. "Those seven guys who came here? Did they tell you their names, give you an address, a phone number, anything?"

"There's a folded piece of paper in the other room," my mother said. "What you need to know is written on that paper."

"What did he promise them in return for their money?" I asked. "Did they tell you any of that?"

My mother nodded. "One of them spoke Italian," she said. "He told me your father had them sign forms, union forms, and told them they would each start to collect a monthly pension as soon as he paid off a few people downtown. People who worked in the pension office."

"Did they show you any of those papers?" I asked.

"One did," she said. "He had them folded in the back pocket of his pants. It didn't mean anything to me. I couldn't understand what was written on them."

I turned and began to walk out of the kitchen toward the living room. My mother reached out and gripped one of my arms. "Where are you going?" she asked.

"To get that sheet of paper," I said. "See if I know any of the names on that list of seven. Then, if they left a number I'll call it and go meet with them. Start to sort this mess out."

"How are you going to do that?" she asked.

"You made it pretty clear it's a debt I need to pay off," I said. "So, what do you care how I do it? All that matters is that it gets done."

"He's hiding out at a hotel in the city," my mother said. "He called just before the men knocked on the door. He told me he's thinking of killing himself."

"It's the same movie all over again," I said. "Every time he pulls a scam and it backfires, he goes into hiding for a while, calls you or me, and says he's going to kill himself. It's just talk. Like one of his cons. Nothing but talk."

I pulled my arm away and walked into the living room and found the folded paper resting in the center of the couch. I picked it up, flipped it open, and read the seven names on the list. I didn't recognize any of them, but I did notice that all of them lived on Long Island, close to where one of my father's sisters lived. "You said we were related to them," I said to my mother. She had followed me into the living room. "How?"

"I recognized the last name," she said. "Your father has relatives with that same last name. They could be cousins. They knew him and had to trust him enough to hand over their money."

"I guess I'll know more after I talk to them," I said. "I'm not going to call from here. I'll use a pay phone. And I'll make sure they don't come up here again and scare you."

"Where are you going to get the money?" my mother asked. Her tone had softened a bit and her anger appeared to have dissipated, replaced more by a sense of sadness.

"That's my worry," I said. "You have your son to worry about. Between that and sitting in the dark and praying, that should keep you plenty busy."

"If I send for this money and give it to you to pay these men, I want you to promise me you will pay me back every nickel," my mother said. "I don't care how long it takes you and what you have to do to earn it. You'll owe that money to me. Every last cent. You pay me a little bit each week, every week. And if you sell a story to one of those magazines you write for, you sign the check over to me."

"It will take me years to pay you back," I said. "I got enough weight on me. The rent and the bills here. The money I give you for shopping. Pocket money so I can get to and from work. I feel like I've been laying out money since I was a kid and I have nothing to show for it."

"I don't care how long it takes you," my mother said. "As long as it's paid back. To the penny. The money doesn't belong to you and it doesn't belong to your father and it doesn't belong to these seven foolish men. The money belongs to my son."

I looked at her, feeling more pity than anger, and I nodded. "I'll pay you back. Soon as I pay off these losers, I'll start working off the debt I owe you. I'll send you money every week. Some you put toward the bills, some toward what I owe you. And I'll keep sending you money for as long as you live. I promise."

My mother tilted her head and reached out a hand for me. I pulled back, shoving the paper with the seven names written on it in the front pocket of my jeans. "What do you mean, send me the money?" she asked. "You can just give it to me."

I shook my head. "I won't be here to give it to you," I said. "I'm done with all of this. I'm moving out. I'm going to find a place of my own. This ends now, with this debt. You want to stay with him, you stay. You want to go, you go. It's up to you now. Me? I'm done."

"Where will you go?" my mother said.

"Anywhere but here," I said. "I won't be able to afford much of a place, but it'll be mine. I don't have it in me anymore to deal with this madness. The two of you have worn me down. Him with his scams and bullshit. You sitting here all day cursing the day you came to America, cursing the day I was born. Blaming your misery on everybody but yourself."

"I did nothing wrong," my mother said.

"You married a man you didn't know, let alone love," I said. "And a cousin on top of it. You came here, and I know it was rough for you and for your son. But you didn't help yourself, either. You didn't learn the language. You didn't go out and find a job. Every nickel that went into your pocket came from him or from me."

"You don't know the full story," my mother said.

"I know enough," I said. "And today I find out even more. That you have a lot of money in Italy and you didn't trust me enough to tell me about it. You only trusted your son. I'm not your son. I'm my father's son. You said it many times when I was a boy, and you say it even more now."

"You are his son," my mother said. "You may not be anything like him, but you are his blood."

"Maybe so," I said. "But when there are bills to be paid or debts to be taken care of or when there's trouble knocking at our door, your son is nowhere to be found," I said. "I'm the one who you expect to clean up the mess. But I'm making it clear now: I'll take your money and pay off these guys. Then I'll pay you off. But that's the end of the line. If another mess happens, don't reach out for me. Call your son if you need help."

My mother glared at me. "Don't forget what I told you," she said. "I want my son's money back. All of it."

"I'll pay you back," I said. "To the very last dime."

I turned away, walked down the narrow corridor, opened the door, and left my mother alone in the apartment.

I SAT ON the front steps of the apartment building, staring up at the elevated subway line less than a quarter of a block away. My arms were braced against my folded knees and I fought back the strong urge to scream or cry. For one of the few times in my life, I felt overwhelmed by what lay in front of me. Forging a career as a writer was difficult enough and maybe was nothing more than a pipe dream. I was making progress, but it was slow and not very steady, and a few scattered clips seemed little more than a tease, not a foundation for bigger and better assignments down the road.

On top of that frustrating feeling was the weight of having to constantly look for money to bail my father out. Until that phone call from my mother, I had actually begun to feel as if the worst of it was behind me. Instead, I was now staring at the biggest financial hurdle of my life. But the deepest wound, the one that struck the hardest, was my mother's revelation that through all our struggles, she had the financial means to bail us out of them and chose not to do so.

I had for many years now come to terms with not being my

mother's favorite child. In some respects, I even understood her reasoning. While I still felt a tinge of sorrow over that fact, there was little I could do to change the way she felt. I shrugged off the comments about how difficult the demands of my half brother's jobs were compared to mine, how challenging it was to deal in the world of big business as opposed to working on a newspaper that people tossed in the garbage when they were through reading it. Those slights had, over time, become easy for me to ignore.

But after that day I would never feel the same toward my mother. I would always love and respect her and do whatever I could to protect her. But this slight, this demand that I pay back a sum of money I barely earned in a year for something my father had done, so she could keep it for her other son, was too much for me to bear, let alone forgive. She had made her choice more than clear to me. There was nothing I could ever do, no achievement I could attain, that would make me rise to the same level as my half brother in her eyes.

In those moments, I was more determined than ever to succeed as a writer. I knew it would not change how she felt about me, but that no longer mattered. I would succeed not because of her but in spite of her. On that day, with her harsh words, she fueled me with the desire to press on, work harder, write better, and not let anything or anyone stand in my way.

That was her gift to me.

I HATED TO leave my mother alone with my father. In my heart I knew nothing good would come of leaving the two of them together. There were problems enough with me standing between them. I could only imagine how much more damage, both financial and physical, my father would bring to bear. But I also knew if I stayed, my presence would encourage him to continue his patterns, depending on me to be there in the end to rescue him. I was hoping that my absence would force my mother to reevaluate her life and situation, that she'd finally break free from her decades of torment and move back to the island where she could once again feel safe.

I also needed to begin a life of my own, to see if I could continue to make inroads in a career that offered me so much hope but also presented so many obstacles. The stories I was eager to tell were about the people and the world I knew, the struggles I had witnessed of a hard-pressed people surviving through their wits and labor.

I also wanted to tell the stories I had heard since I was a child. Some of the tales were harsh, a few funny, and all of them very real. My mother was an important part of that equation. The stories she told and the life she led were not unique to her. They were lived by thousands just like her. And while she often spoke to me in a negative tone, that only reinforced my determination to put those stories to paper. To succeed and to prove her doubts and fears about me were misguided.

It was not an easy journey, nor did I expect it to be. I had been promoted to entertainment reporter at the *Daily News* and during my time there used each story to find my own identity as a writer. I would profile authors on a regular basis, hoping to take from the interview as much of their knowledge as I could absorb.

I also fell in love, married, and became a father while I worked at the paper. I moved on to magazines and then hit a wall with such force that it made me question why I had ever considered the career path I had chosen. I'd left the paper for a Time Inc. magazine. During those years, that company was considered the gold standard of magazines, one that could set me on my way to a lucrative career path. Instead, the magazine I was hired to write for crashed and burned after only nine months and led to a six-year odyssey of working at start-up magazines, temporary work on special issues, and a freelance life I was ill-suited for, earning money writing for publications that, more often than not, were read in prisons.

I still sent money to my mother each week during these years and would visit her as often as I could. My father had been slowed by illness and seemed to focus more on his health than on scamming innocent people out of money. The violence in him had not abated, however, and it seemed as if it never would. At least, not until his death.

On one of my visits, I was walking with my mother as she headed for a weekday mass, stealing a few moments away from my father.

"I'm sorry you didn't bring the baby with you," she said. "I would have liked to see her."

"She's fighting a cold," I said. "Again. She gets so many colds this time of year."

It was early December, a few weeks before Christmas, and the wind whipped around the elevated steel beams of the IRT subway line on White Plains Road. "She takes after you, then," my mother said. "When you were her age, the doctor was at our apartment every week, sometimes even twice. No matter what we did, you were always sick."

"I didn't think he came for me," I said. "I thought he was pulling some medical scams with Dad."

"Maybe he was doing both," she said. "That part I don't know. The part about you being sick is what I remember."

"I'll bring her up next time," I said.

"Where are you working now?" my mother asked. "Last time we talked, that magazine you were working for went out of business."

"I freelance now," I said. "It means I work for myself. If a magazine wants one of my stories, then they hire me to write for them."

"And you make a living doing this?"

"Not a very good one," I said. "Some months are better than others, and most months are even worse. Some days I think you were right about that bank job I got right after high school. Maybe that was as good as it was going to get for me."

"What does that mean?" she asked. "You're going to quit? No more writing stories? You always told me that's all you wanted to do with your life. If that's not true, then, yes, maybe you should have kept the job working at that bank."

"I don't know," I said. "No one seems to want my stories. Not the places where you want them to be wanted, anyway. I'm just going around in circles and getting nowhere fast."

"Good thing your wife works," my mother said. "At least there's one check coming in every week."

"She's doing very well," I said. "Just got a big promotion. It can't be a good feeling for her, married to somebody just scraping by."

"I don't know anything about the world you travel in," my mother said. "But maybe you're just not telling the stories you need to tell, the stories you know that no one else does. Those are the ones you should write. Maybe those are the ones people would pay you for."

"What stories are you talking about?" I asked.

"The ones you've heard and the ones you've seen with your own eyes," my mother said. "Your father killed his first wife and he went to prison for it. That makes you the son of a killer. That's just one. All those stories I told you about the war and how brave and tough the people had to be in order to survive and still so many died. There are so many stories there. The people of the neighborhoods we lived in, their lives, their struggles. Maybe somebody needs to tell their stories. And that somebody could be you."

"It could be nobody wants those stories," I said. "And right now, whether they want them or not, I can't get anywhere near the people who are in a position to let me write them."

"I can't help you with that," she said. "The doors to a better life for people like us are always closed. We have to push against them again and again until they open. I could never get my door open. I've been stuck in the same place for more years than I want to remember. I'll say a prayer that for you it will be different. That maybe you will be the one to open that door."

We stopped in front of the church and my mother turned to face me. "There's something I need to tell you before you go," she said. "Something I've been thinking about for a long time. I've wanted to tell you each time I see you, but one thing or another always seems to get in our way."

"What is it?" I asked. "Are you sick?"

She shook her head. "Nothing like that," she said. "I know you've always been afraid of being like your father. I worried about it, too, for a lot of years. You're his son and, yes, every time I look at you, I see his face. That part's not going to change. But you are nothing like your father and you never were. You probably know that by now. But I think it's important that you hear it from me. You are not your father. That's one worry at least that you can put aside."

I kissed her cheek, cold and red from the brisk wind, and waited as she made her way up the steps of the church. She opened a thick door and slowly stepped inside the darkness of a place she had come to think of as her second home and disappeared.

AS I WALKED up the stairs to the IRT line and the long ride home, I thought back to that first summer I spent in Ischia and a story my mother had told me. She had come over for a short visit and the two of us were walking together on a beach less than a quarter of a mile from the house she had grown up in. "My sisters tell me you have made many friends in the weeks you've been here," my mother said.

"Yes," I said. "Everybody's been really nice."

"But you need to be careful, too," my mother said.

"Careful about what?"

"About what you take from other people," she said.

"This isn't another one of your stories about bodies coming out of a wall and dragging me off to hell, is it?" I asked.

"No," she said. "This is worse. Because this can really happen to you."

"What is it?"

"It's called La Fattura," my mother said. "I'm not sure myself if it's a drug or a curse or you're put under a trance. Either way, you cannot let it happen to you."

"Who is going to do that to me?" I asked.

"It could be anyone," she said. "Some new friend you made. A friendly face sitting next to you in a club or a bar. You will never know where it comes from and who the messenger is."

"So, what do you want me to do?" I asked. "If I don't know it's coming, how can I stop it?"

"There's one simple rule to follow," she said. "Whenever you are in the company of people you don't know or in a house you've never been in before, you need to be on your guard. Especially if they offer you something to eat or drink."

"You mean it's like a poison?"

"If they offer you food or a glass of anything, even water, say no," my mother continued. "Especially if no one else is eating or drinking the same food or from the same bottle."

"Okay," I said. "I guess I can do that."

"You *must* do it," she said. "Otherwise, you can end up anywhere and be living with a woman you barely know."

"I'm fourteen, Mom," I said. "I don't think any woman is out looking to live with me."

"You'd be surprised," my mother said. "You'd be very surprised. It has happened here many times before."

"Did it happen to anybody you know?"

"Yes, my brother," my mother said. "And that's how he ended up married to his wife. He was on his honeymoon in Florence, visiting our sister. He was sitting in the kitchen when he suddenly shook his head and asked, 'Am I in your house? In Florence?' My sister looked back at him and nodded. He then asked, 'Why did I come here? I should be in Ischia.' My sister thought he was joking and told him he was there on his honeymoon with his new wife. My brother stood up, his body drenched in sweat, shaking. 'I'm married,' he said in a loud voice. 'Who did I marry? Do I know her? Is she here?' He then collapsed back in his chair and closed his eyes. He had taken a drink offered to him by a stranger and ended up a married man. He was a victim of La Fattura."

We walked in silence for several moments, both of us watching as the waves brushed over our feet. I then looked up at her and asked, "Do you really believe any of that?"

My mother smiled and shrugged. "It might be true," she said. "But it sure is a good story to tell, no?"

"A very good story," I said, returning the smile.

"And just to be safe, in case it is true, don't drink or eat anything given to you by anyone you don't know," she said.

"You can count on that," I said. "I might not take anything from people I do know."

"Even better," my mother said.

1990-2004

❦

MY MOTHER FINALLY did move back to Ischia, to live on the island she always thought of as home, shortly after my father's death from bone cancer in 1988. She lived in one of the two apartments left to her by my Nonna Maria, a one-bedroom with a small garden. I was pretty sure she received several pension checks and Social Security, but I was never told for certain, nor did I ever ask. As always, my mother's financial situation was kept between her and my half brother. Still, I sent her money every week, as I had done every week of my life for as far back as my memory takes me.

We spoke by phone a few times a week and she sounded much more relaxed, less fearful, and much less timid than when she had lived in New York. She was back in her comfort zone, and the realization was slowly taking root that no further harm would come her way.

Her move to Ischia coincided with my writing career taking a turn for the better. I landed my first TV job in 1988, working on a syndicated series. That, in turn, led to a five-year stint as the managing editor of the CBS series *Top Cops*. I also sold my first book— about my father and the murder he committed in 1946. I was by now the father of two children, happily married to a successful woman, a homeowner, and free of debt.

The day I made that first book deal, I called my mother in Ischia and told her the news. For a few brief moments there was silence on her end of the phone. "You found someone to pay you to write about your father," she said. "I think he would be happy to know that. I also think he would ask you for half the money they are giving you."

"And gamble the other half away," I said.

"They made fun of us all those years," my mother said. "We suffered and had to pay off his debts, and to them—his friends, his family—it was all one big joke. It was almost as if they took pleasure from what we had to go through."

"Those days are past us now, Mom," I said. "They can't touch you anymore. And neither can he."

"But the memories are still there," my mother said. "You can't live as many years as I did with all I went through and shrug it away. Those years living in those humid apartments, those cement floors, stay with you. All those beatings we both took can't be tossed aside because you are writing a book or working on a television show."

"Do you remember the night I spent in the hospital, at Saint Clare's?" I asked. "I think I was about nine, maybe ten years old. My head was bandaged, and I couldn't see out of one of my eyes."

"Yes," my mother said. "I remember. You still have a scar over your eye where they had to stitch your wound closed. And your head was bandaged because you needed to be stitched in three different places."

"The room was dark and had a weird smell to it," I said. "We were alone in the room and you sat close to me on the bed, holding my hand."

"You were afraid to go to sleep," my mother said. "And you didn't like being in a hospital."

"Not many people do," I said. "Especially a kid. So you stayed up all night and told me stories. I don't remember how I got to the hospital. But I do remember every one of those stories you told me."

"You stepped in front of me," my mother said. "That's how you ended up in the hospital. The beating was meant for me, and you stood in front of him and told him to stop. And so he took it out on you instead. It was the first time you had done that."

"Do you remember the stories you told me?" I asked.

"Some of them," my mother said. "You laughed at the one about my father having my brothers give him his weekly shave. He would keep loose change in his shirt pockets, and my brothers would lather up his face and then manage to get some soap in his eyes while they took the change from his pocket."

"That's right," I said. "And Nonno would say to them, 'I don't understand, you don't need to shave my eyes, just my face. There's no reason to put soap anywhere near them.' "

My mother laughed. "My father loved every minute of it," she said. "Those were simpler times. It seemed so much easier to laugh back then. He was planning to give them the change anyway, but he let them have their fun."

"And then you told me about the bombing raids on Ischia," I said. "Where you and your brothers were almost killed."

"My brother Mario saved us both," she said. "Me and Joseph. The bombs that night came so suddenly, and we were still a few blocks from our home. We started to run, and Joseph fell and hit his head against a stone wall. I tripped turning back to help him. Mario came racing toward us, lifted Joseph from the ground, and wrapped his arms around both of us and didn't stop and didn't let go until we were all safe. He was just a little boy. But he kept saying to us both, 'Don't worry. Their bombs won't hurt us. I promise you.' "

"That's why Uncle Mario still has those nightmares," I said. "I was there for a few of them. It's almost as if he's reliving that bombing raid. All these years later and he remembers it as if it were yesterday."

"Those moments never leave you," my mother said. "No matter how many years have passed."

I paused for a moment. "Thanks, Mom," I said. "I never took the time to thank you, and I should have. I'm sorry for that."

"Thank me for what?" my mother asked.

"For all the stories you told me," I said. "For taking me to those great Italian movies when I was a kid. I still watch them every few months, especially the ones by De Sica and anything with Anna Magnani in it."

"I never think of them as just movies," she said. "Watching them seems so real to me. The reason I think they were able to tell those stories so well was because they had lived that life, those moments."

"And for taking me to the wrestling matches once a month," I said. "You and those other crazy Italian women, everyone believing what they were seeing was real. I got my son, Nick, into watching wrestling with me now. It's not the same as it was when you and I went. The guys are bigger, louder, but it's still fun to sit and watch with him. Makes me think of our time together."

"He'll learn from it, like you did," she said. "There was always a story to every match, and the stories usually had happy endings. A little different than real life."

"I even have fond memories of sitting there and watching Perry Como with you," I said. "Christmas and Easter aren't the same without him."

"I wasn't the best mother for you," she said, her voice close to cracking. "I wish it could have been different, but a lot of it was out of my control. There were many days and nights when I didn't think we would make it out. But here we are. You in New York and me in Ischia. Still breathing. I'm sure there's a story somewhere in there, too. I'm just too old and tired to tell it. So I'll leave that one to you to pass on."

I told her I loved her and hung up the phone. I sat in the quiet darkness of my home office, my eyes closed, listening to a hard rain land against the side of the windows. Against the hardest of odds, with practically no one there to help her, my mother had survived. And I hoped that knowing that would provide her with some level of comfort. She had more than earned it.

THE CALL CAME early on a Saturday morning. It was my cousin Paola from Florence. She was emotional and spoke in a rapid tone. "Your mother was very sick," she said. "She was diagnosed in Ischia, and she came here to Florence at her doctor's suggestion for a second opinion."

"I just talked to her last week," I said. "She didn't sound sick."

"The doctors here saw her on Thursday and confirmed what Agostino had diagnosed her with in Ischia," Paola said. "She went out shopping for a dress yesterday with my mother, something nice for her to be buried in."

"Buried in?" I said. "What does she have, Paola?"

"Lung cancer," Paola said. "Very advanced. There was nothing any doctor could do to help her."

I froze for a brief moment. "What are you telling me?" I asked. "What do you mean there was nothing to do?"

"She died this morning," Paola said. "She had breakfast and went into the living room to lay down on the couch. And that's where she died."

I pulled the phone from my ear and made a vain attempt to stay calm. In Italy, burial has to occur within twenty-four hours of death. There would be no way for me to get on a plane and to Florence in time for her funeral. "Are you asking the church for extra time?" I said. "So she can be brought to Ischia to be buried there?"

"No," Paola said. "She'll be buried here, in Florence, along with members of our family. Your brother thinks that's for the best."

"My brother?" I said. "Did you call him before you called me?"

"Your brother is on his way," Paola said. "He should be here in a few hours."

"When did he know?" I asked.

"When did he know what?" Paola asked.

"When did he know she was sick?" I asked. "And when did he know she was on her way to Florence?"

"He's always known," Paola said. "Your mother told him."

I stood there shaking my head, feeling a combination of anger, resentment, and resignation. "Thanks for letting me know," I said, and hung up the phone.

I sat in my home-office chair and thought about my mother. She used to always say, "Born in Ischia. Die in Ischia." But that turned out not to be the case. She would be buried in a city not her own after having spent decades in a country she never thought of as home. To this day, I have visited my mother's grave only once, when I found myself in Florence on a magazine assignment. I was brought there by a cousin and couldn't even tell you the name of the cemetery. It seemed strange to see her framed photo mounted on a marble wall, surrounded by those to whom she bore no connection. I suppose it's a fitting final resting place for her, since she spent so much of her life living among people with whom she shared nothing but an address.

I did not like it then and like it even less now how she kept the news of her illness from me, preferring to confide only in her other son. But, looking back, I learned of her death the way she wanted me to. My mother had long feared being a burden to her children, and she was aware of the sacrifices that had been made by others on her behalf. In my case, most of those sacrifices were financial. Money was what she counted on me to deliver. Emotional support, maybe even a deeper love than she could feel for me, she sought from my half brother.

I was not her favorite child. And I was a child she had likely never wanted. But despite that difficult truth, I never once doubted my mother's love for me.

She gave me the strength to strive for what I wanted. Her anger was my fuel. Her desperation to get out of the life she found herself in matched my own desires to escape that very world.

Her stories will always stay with me, and I've put many of them to good use. Her negative attacks on me drove me all that much harder to prove her wrong. My mother never got to live the life she deserved. She got very little happiness in her time. The laughs and the pleasant moments were spread thin, not enough to satisfy. She suffered at the hands of others and often lashed out at the one who stood by her side. She was not sentimental in the way most mothers are, she was never easy to please, and she was stubborn to the point of exasperation. Her beliefs were set in stone, no matter how hurtful they often were. She was a deeply religious woman yet cursed and condemned all those who had done her harm.

She was my mother, Raffaela Carcaterra.

She was born in 1922, the year Benito Mussolini first took charge of Italy, and she died of lung cancer in March of 2004. She always sought a peaceful life. It was all she ever truly wanted. It was what she spent many a worrisome day and many a painful night wishing for. I hope now that my mother has finally found that well-deserved peace.

SUSAN

1976–1979

❧

I REMEMBER THE first time I saw her as if it were an hour ago.

I was on the seventh floor of the New York *Daily News* building, the old one, at 220 East 42nd Street. It was early October 1976, and I was wrapping up my first week working as a copy boy at the paper. It was early into my 5-P.M.-TO-1-A.M. shift and I was leaning against a cold wall, waiting for the next elevator to arrive. The bell from the car on the far right rang, and the doors slid open and she walked out.

She was short and pretty, with brown curly hair and a face that was hard to ignore. She was wearing a white T-shirt, a brown leather jacket, and tight jeans, the pants legs tucked inside the tops of red cowboy boots. I looked at her and nodded. She glanced at me and smiled. She turned and headed past the reception desk, toward the back of the editorial department, where the entertainment and feature sections were located.

That first moment has stayed with me all these years.

It isn't because there was a love-at-first-sight spark or that the moment was anything more than what it was—two people exchanging a look that lasted less than a second. Neither of us had any way of knowing that first meeting would lead to sharing a life together for thirty-four years. We would have two children and love each other, argue, laugh, cry, struggle, and succeed. She would become the very best friend I ever had, the one person I trusted more than any other.

She would become the most important person in my life.

But on that day, in front of that seventh-floor elevator, neither one of us could imagine any of that. That day, for the two of us, was nothing more than a brief moment between two strangers.

I DID NOT see her again for several months. In that time, she went from freelance music columnist to on-staff entertainment editor. Her column ran every Sunday, with her name in bold black letters in the middle of the copy.

Susan Toepfer.

Those years were not easy ones for women working on newspapers, especially one like the *Daily News*. It was a very male-dominated paper, run by a squadron of editors and reporters who worked long hours and spent more time in the local drinking hole—Costello's—than they did at home.

There were a handful of female reporters on staff and a scattering of woman editors, mostly working out of the features department. With one or two exceptions, hard news was considered a male domain, and the term "political correctness" had yet to come into vogue. Even if it had, the phrase would have been ignored in that smoke-drenched city room, where the desks were occupied by middle-aged white men filled with swagger, bravado, and booze.

The week Susan was due to start her new role, a memo was tacked on various bulletin boards around the office complaining that there were too many women being hired at the paper and naming her as the prime example. I stood in front of one of those boards and read the memo and scanned the signatures attached to it. To my right, another copy boy simply shook his head. "You believe this shit?" he asked. "Somebody putting up a memo like that? I don't get it. What the hell are they so afraid of?"

"It's not all of them," I said. "The guys who signed this are just the loudest of the bunch."

"They treat *everybody* the same," he said. "Like shit. Last night I had to drive one of the editors back home. He was so drunk he could barely get in the back seat. Lived somewhere in Westchester County. I needed to pull over twice so he could throw up."

"You know anything about her?" I asked, my eyes still on the memo. "I mean, other than the column she writes every week."

"I talked to her a few times," he said. "She stops by Costello's now and then, usually with her editor. She's nice enough. A little shy maybe, or arrogant—hard to tell. She seems a little young to be the entertainment editor."

"She might be good," I said, starting to walk away.

"Even if she is, it won't matter to the guys in the city room," he said. "They see what they want to see. They don't want to see a woman working next to them any more than they want to see one of us be made a reporter."

OVER THE NEXT few months, Susan settled into her new job, and I was moved from night shift to days and then, eventually, into the features department as a movie-timetable clerk.

In that role, I got to see Susan every day, although it was from a safe distance and we barely spoke. I never ventured into her office, and she only came out of hers to hand copy to an assistant or layouts to an art director. The only opportunity I had to even exchange pleasantries with her was at the coffee cart, which stopped by the features department every afternoon at four—and even that was a reach.

Other than the fact that we worked on the same floor for the same newspaper, we had little in common. We weren't friends, and I would have been surprised if she even knew my name. While I still very much remembered that first look and smile we'd shared months ago by the elevator bank, I had serious doubts that the moment even registered in her mind.

My first attempts to speak to her while we waited on the coffee line were, at best, awkward. There was a pecking order at the *Daily News*, and I was, if not at the very bottom of that order, close enough to it to be nearly invisible to those above me. Susan was an editor, an executive, and there was an unspoken understanding that only idle chatter was acceptable between our two levels. To make the situation worse, I was painfully aware of how inept I was at making small talk, especially with someone I didn't know well. I could talk deep into the night with close friends and relatives. But put me next to a stranger in any type of social setting and I had difficulty forming coherent sentences. I remember the time I was in a coffee line, barely a week into my copy boy's job, when I turned and saw Jimmy Breslin standing behind me. It was the first time I had seen him up close, and right there and then, my mind filled with all the books and columns of his that I had read and studied and could practically recite out loud. "I'm in a rush," Breslin said. "Do me a favor and grab me a Sanka?"

I stared at him for what had to be a matter of seconds but felt more like hours. "What do you want me to do with it?" was all I could manage to stammer.

"You drink Sanka?" he asked.

I shook my head.

"Then, bring it to me," Breslin said as he started to walk away. "Because I do. If you can manage that, I'll pay for it and for whatever you do drink."

I was in front of Susan on the coffee line. I turned and smiled at her. "You want to move ahead of me?" I asked.

Susan shook her head. "That's okay," she said. "The line moves pretty fast."

"I buy a cup every afternoon," I said. "And I don't even like the coffee."

"So why do you do it?"

"I'm a movie-timetable clerk," I said. "Twenty-eight pages a day of what movie's playing where and when. I'll do anything to get away from the typewriter for a few minutes. So I come running soon as I see the cart arrive. Helps break up the day."

"Sounds pretty boring," she said.

"You don't know the half of it," I said.

She smiled and said, "There's no reason for me to know."

I felt incredibly nervous and was sweating over every word I spoke, knowing the last thing a busy editor needed to hear were the travails of a timetable clerk. It was as if every word I spoke lowered any opinion she might have had of me, assuming she even had one. But I found it hard to take my eyes off her. I very much wanted to make a good impression but knew I was failing miserably.

"No," I said, turning away from her. "I guess not."

The line inched up a few feet, and I put my hands in the pockets of my jeans and looked at her and smiled. "How are you liking the new job?" I asked.

"It's been okay so far," she said. "And after hearing about your job, I have nothing to complain about."

"I know you need a lot of stories each week to fill up the section," I said. "I notice you've been using freelancers on some of the articles. Is that a regular thing you'll be doing?"

She looked at me and gave me a half smile. "You're next on line," she said, not bothering to answer my question.

"Right," I said, turning to place my order. "Somebody somewhere might be looking to go to a movie tonight, and they'll need to know what time it starts."

IT WAS DIFFICULT for someone in my position to get a real assignment at the paper in those years. The newspaper guild would not allow editors to approach anyone but a reporter with a story suggestion, which left me out. Since the paper was staffed up, you couldn't go to an editor and pitch a story idea, because he could then easily assign it to one of the writers working the entertainment beat. You had to find an idea to pitch that no one could be assigned or would suggest. You had to find stories the on-staff reporters were either not aware of or would not consider bringing up in a meeting.

Despite the difficulty, I had been able to break through and publish a few stories as a copy boy and timetable clerk. Martin Scorsese, then in the early years of his career, had directed a documentary about his parents called *Italianamerican*. I read about it and went to see the daily entertainment editor and proposed doing a story on Scorsese's mother and father. I gambled that no one on staff would be interested in interviewing his Italian American parents. My gamble paid off.

I was assigned the piece and it ran a few weeks after I wrote it. I then found out that Scorsese was planning a movie on the life of former middleweight boxing champion Jake LaMotta. The movie, *Raging Bull,* had not yet started filming, so for me, the timing was perfect. Editors love to have stories they can "bank"—have ready for down-the-road placement. The LaMotta piece gave my editor an article he could run whenever he had a slot that needed to be filled.

Getting into the daily paper got me some attention, but I knew the big prize was landing a piece in the Sunday entertainment section, then called "Leisure." At the time, daily circulation at the paper hovered around two million. But Sunday circulation passed north of three million, and the Sunday paper was read by every editor on staff. Other than writing for the magazine or the op-ed pages, there was no better way for a writer to get noticed than having a piece run in the Sunday entertainment section.

I had not talked to Susan since that first awkward encounter by the coffee cart. The few times we crossed paths in the halls, she either seemed distracted or simply ignored me as she walked past. But I had come across a story idea I thought would be perfect for the Sunday section. All I needed was to somehow convince an editor who barely acknowledged my existence that it was indeed a good idea and that I was the right person to write the piece. I fretted for a week over how to approach Susan without getting rejected.

"Every time Susan Toepfer passes by, she always makes a point of saying hello and even stops to talk to you," I said to my best friend on the paper, Hank, at one point during that week. "She never does that with me."

"Maybe that's because she likes me," Hank said, smiling. "Or maybe she doesn't like you."

"You might be right," I said. "I tried talking to her once and that went over like a fart in a space suit."

"She's still pretty new here," Hank said. "And not everybody has greeted her with open arms. Maybe she's trying to figure out who wants her here and who doesn't."

"I have an idea for a Sunday piece," I said. "But I need to pitch it to her, and I'm not even sure she'll let me in her office. You know if any of the guys have tried to get an assignment from her?"

Hank nodded. "One or two," he said. "But nothing came of it. She let her assistant write a few pieces, but he's on her staff."

"How about you?" I asked. "You run anything by her?"

Hank smiled again. "I told you she likes me," he said. "Why ruin a good thing?"

"I'm going to go in Monday morning and take my shot," I said.

"Is it a good idea?" Hank asked.

"It's about the Three Stooges," I said.

"Seriously?" Hank said.

"Yeah, why?"

"I don't know," Hank said. "She doesn't seem like a Three Stooges kind of girl. I could be wrong. I guess we'll have our answer Monday morning. I might be in a little late, so wait for me before you go see her. I don't want to miss it."

"You think she's going to say no, don't you?" I asked.

"Odds are she'll take a pass," Hank said. "I don't know her well, but I would bet money she has never had a conversation about the Three Stooges in her life. You might even get a smile out of her, before she asks you to get out of her office."

"Or hits me with her ashtray," I said.

MONDAY MORNING, THE door to her office was open. She was sitting at her desk, still catching up with the morning papers, a hot cup of coffee resting just beyond her right elbow. The office was small, with a desk, a computer, two chairs, and a large wall calendar, where she had written the dates of Broadway openings, TV premieres, and movie releases. A full-length window looked down at 42nd Street between Second and Third Avenue. She was wearing a thin purple blouse, with the first two buttons undone, and several bracelets were wrapped around each wrist. I knocked gently against the door and waited for her to look up.

"You got a minute?" I asked.

Susan nodded and I walked in and stood in front of her. "Sit down if you like," she said.

I sat in the chair closest to the window, took a quick glance outside, and then looked back at Susan, who was now leaning back in her leather chair, her hands curled around the cup of coffee. "I have an idea for your section," I said. "It's not going to happen for another month, so there's plenty of time to get it written and put on the schedule."

"It must be a good story," she said. "Since you already have it on the schedule."

"It is," I said. "Or will be, once I write it."

"Let's hear it, then," she said, taking a sip of her coffee.

"Channel Eleven is running a Three Stooges marathon weekend next month," I said. "Showing all their movies, the ones with Curly and the ones with Shemp."

"And I would want a story on the Three Stooges because . . ."

"Because our readers would love it," I said. "I grew up watching them, and so did many of the people who buy the paper. They know more about the Curly Shuffle than about Jane Austen."

"Are any of them around for you to interview?" she asked.

"No," I said. "And I wouldn't want to, anyway. I'd like to write an essay about them, what they meant to me growing up and why they mattered as much as they did."

Susan stared at me for a moment, then rested her coffee cup on her desk and glanced out her window. "I won't assign it," she said as she turned back to look at me. "I'm not sure if it's a good idea or not, but that's not why I'm not assigning it to you."

"Then why?"

"I don't know if you can write," she said. "And I have no idea if you can deliver an essay. But that doesn't mean you *can't* write it. If you do, let me read it, and we'll go from there."

I nodded. "If that's your best offer," I said, "I'll take it."

"It's my only offer," she said, smiling.

I stood and glanced down at her. "How soon do you need it?" I asked. "For it to make the issue?"

"*If* it's going to make the issue, I'd like to have it a week from today," Susan said. "If you need a few days more, take them, but not too many more. It would need to run the Sunday before marathon weekend. Again, *if* it's going to run."

I smiled. "Got it," I said. "I'll have it done by this time next week. Thanks for giving me a shot."

"I haven't given you anything," Susan said, returning to the morning papers. "You're the one that's taking the shot."

I started to head out of the office and then stopped and looked back at her. She gazed up at me. "I know some of the staff haven't given you a warm welcome," I said. "Don't take it personal. They treat everybody who hasn't been here for more than twenty years like shit."

"I don't plan on being here for twenty years," Susan said.

"Promise you'll stick around at least another week," I said. "Until I get my essay on your desk."

Susan nodded and smiled. "A chance to read a personal essay about the Three Stooges?" she said. "That will get me through another week."

I WROTE AND rewrote the essay at least a dozen times.

I sat at the kitchen table in the East Bronx apartment I shared with my parents and worked on the piece from the end of one of my shifts until the start of the next. I worked in silence, while my parents slept, the only light a small lamp in the center of the table. The only noise came from the elevated subway running throughout the night half a block from our apartment. I stopped working only to shower, eat, and put in a few calls to the publicity department at Channel 11, to have them send me the press kit on the Three Stooges marathon.

I knew the marathon would get a solid viewership. These were the years before cable, streaming, Netflix, and binge-watching. There were only seven channels New Yorkers could tune in to, and Channel 11 was the most popular of the local stations.

I decided to take a risk and make the essay a personal one—writing about what the Three Stooges meant to me as a child growing up in a railroad tenement apartment in Hell's Kitchen. I would watch their antics most afternoons after school before running off to either play with friends or head to the nearby public library to do my homework and read books by my favorite authors—Alexandre Dumas, Victor Hugo, and Jack London. As for many others my age, the Stooges were a childhood staple and left in their wake many fine memories.

They were a welcome break from the daily battles waged between the walls of our apartment by my parents. The slapstick violence of the Stooges was comical and innocent, unlike the violence faced inside the rooms I lived in. Their exploits were a welcome respite from reality, the difficulties and dangers they faced all happily solved within one short episode.

The Stooges also reminded me of the men I knew from the two neighborhoods I was raised in—Hell's Kitchen and the East Bronx. Like them, the Stooges were dreamers, always desperate to find the next dollar to keep them going for another day. They dreamed up foolish schemes that were destined to fail, but despite those failings they always came back with yet another crazy con. I grew up surrounded by Stooges. The only difference was, the ones I watched on television always brought a smile to my face.

While I was working on the essay, I thought back to the seven summers I had spent on the island of Ischia in Italy with my Nonna Maria. She always believed I would one day be able to tell stories of my own, ones that mattered to me and that I could then share with others. She had never read a book or bothered with the daily papers and didn't know anyone who made their living telling stories. But she had a faith in me and a strong belief that I somehow would be able to figure a way to achieve my goal.

This essay would be the first step. I was determined to not let Nonna Maria down.

I arrived at the paper early Monday morning, wanting to get in before Susan got to her office. I didn't want to hand her the article and risk having her read it in front of me. I thought it best if Susan sought me out to render her verdict. The door to her office was locked, so I slid the large white envelope containing my essay under her door and went to my desk to begin my workday.

I did my best to not think about what her reaction to the piece might be, but all I could do *was* think about it, all through that morning and into the afternoon. I avoided looking toward her office or making eye contact when she walked past my desk. I didn't even know if she would get to the piece that day and began to wonder if she would bother to read it at all.

I spent most of the day typing up the movie times for Tuesday's edition for theaters in the five boroughs. Hank did the same for Westchester, Suffolk, and Nassau counties. "How come they don't give us New Jersey to do, too?" Hank asked, trying to get my mind off the essay.

"That's all we need," I said. "Another hundred theaters to include. We're losing enough brain cells."

Hank looked around, his eyes scanning the rear of the features department, where Susan's office was situated, and then turned back to me. "A month ago, I filled in for her assistant for three days, and Mondays are when she reads pieces that came in over the weekend," he said. "She'll read yours. If she said she would, then she will."

"I'm not worried about her reading it," I said. "I'm worried about her liking it. I don't know what I was thinking. First piece I write for her is about the Three Stooges? She must have written me off as a loser as soon as she heard the idea."

"You wrote what you wanted to write," Hank said. "But, to be safe, don't make the next story you pitch about Soupy Sales."

"There won't be a second story if I strike out on this one," I said.

"You don't know that," Hank said. "She can pass on the piece for a lot of reasons. Could be because she doesn't have space to run it, too many assigned articles running that week. Maybe one of the city editors vetoes the piece because he hates the Stooges."

"How can anybody hate the Stooges?" I said, smiling for the first time that day.

"Hard to believe, I know," Hank said. "But there is always that one guy who just can't grasp their sophisticated humor."

"Or that one editor," I said.

BY THAT FRIDAY, I still hadn't heard from Susan. At the end of my shift, I shut down my computer, eager to bring an end to a tedious and nerve-racking week. I was the last of the clerks to leave, my mind less on movie timetables and more on the fact that five days had gone by and not a word from Susan.

I was so buried in my own thoughts I didn't hear her walk up behind me. "You got a few minutes?" she asked. "If you're in a rush, it can wait until Monday."

I turned to face her and shook my head. "I have time," I said.

"Great," she said. "I'm going to run down to the lobby and get a soda. Can I get you anything?"

"No, thanks," I said. "I'm good."

Susan started walking toward the elevators. "I'll meet you in my office," she said. "Grab a seat and relax."

I sat in one of the two chairs facing her desk and stared out at the street traffic below. Susan walked in, holding a Diet Coke with a straw slid into the opening, and sat in her leather chair. "Sorry it took me so long to get to your piece," she said. "Been a crazy week."

"No problem," I said. "You have more pages to fill than any editor on the floor. To me, it looks like a ton of fun, but I'm not the one who has to assign the stories and fill the pages."

Susan turned to her computer and clicked a few keys. "I have to admit you surprised me," she said. "I don't know what I was expecting, reading an essay about the Three Stooges. But I do know what I wasn't expecting."

"What's that?"

"That it would be good," she said. "I mean very good. You did a terrific job. I'm going to run it next Sunday. I need to pull a few photos. Would it be okay if I ran them by you? We can pick the best one to fit the piece."

I nodded and smiled. "I would like that," I said.

"It doesn't need much editing," Susan said. "Some tightening here and there and a few cuts. We can do it now if you like, get it ready for layout on Monday."

"What do you need me to do?" I asked.

"Step over behind me," she said. "You read over my shoulder and we'll go over the edits I'd like to make. You have a problem with any, speak up."

I walked over and stood behind her chair and saw my article on her computer screen. Her edits were smooth, deft, and on the mark. As I watched her make the changes, I saw her smile at some of the lines I had written. "You have a nice style to your writing, a nice rhythm. You might want to think about writing a book or a script at some point."

Up until that moment, no one, especially not an editor, had ever said anything like that to me. I was silent for a while, not knowing what to say, not knowing how to respond to such a generous compliment. "Thank you" was all I could manage. I fought to contain the happiness and excitement I felt, hearing those words, believing, for the first time, that I was now on the right track, that what I wanted to achieve was more than just a foolish fantasy, that I could indeed make it happen. At that moment, I thought of Nonna Maria and knew that she, too, would be pleased.

It took Susan less than fifteen minutes to walk me through her edits, all of which made the essay that much better. She clicked on the save button and turned away from her computer. She looked up at me and smiled. "If every story was as easy to edit as yours, this job would be a dream," she said.

"I appreciate you letting me write the piece," I said. "I know it would have been easier to just say no, and it means a lot to me you didn't."

"Isn't this the part where you ask me if I'm going to pay you for the piece?" Susan said. "And how much?"

"It probably is," I said. "But I'm not going to ask you that. Not tonight. All I want tonight is a glass of wine and a quiet place to drink it. Best way I can think of to end a great day."

Susan glanced at her watch. "The Oyster Bar at Grand Central," she said. "It's usually empty this time of night. That's as quiet a place as you're going to find around here."

"Is that where you go?" I asked. "When you're looking for a quiet place?"

Susan nodded. "Costello's is fun, but it's too loud and everyone from work drinks there," she said. "The only ones you find drinking at the Oyster Bar at night are commuters who missed their train."

"We could go together," I said. "I mean, if you're done for the night. My treat."

Susan looked at me and tilted her head slightly. "I thought you said you wanted to drink a glass of wine in a quiet place," she said.

"I did," I said. "But I never said I wanted to drink it alone."

"I've been warned on more than one occasion that editors and clerks should not socialize," Susan said, standing and reaching for a jacket hanging around her chair.

I shook my head. "You shouldn't and you wouldn't be," I said. "Tonight, I'm a writer and you're my editor, and from what I've read and what I've seen around here, they drink together all the time."

THE ESSAY ON the Stooges was published on a Sunday. By the end of that first week, more than sixty readers had called the paper to express how much they liked it, and close to the same amount sent in letters expressing the same sentiments. Editors stopped to compliment me on the piece, as did some of the reporters whose names I recognized only from their bylines. Jimmy Breslin teased me about the attention I was getting. "Follow that up with a piece on Abbott and Costello and you might end up with your own column," he told me.

I was even invited to a luncheon by the local chapter of the Three Stooges fan club, where I would be made an honorary Stooge. "I don't know how you can pass up such an honor," Hank said, as soon as he heard the news. "Who needs a Pulitzer when you can be an honorary Stooge?"

"They said I could bring a guest," I said. "Was going to ask Susan."

"You should," he said. "She's probably sitting in her office thinking, 'Yes, I'm a Tony Award voter and can go to all the screenings I want and every publisher in town sends me every book they want reviewed, but there's still something missing.' A lunch where she can see you named an honorary Stooge—what woman wouldn't want that?"

"If she says no, you're next on my list."

"She's better-looking than me," Hank said. "But I would be the better date."

"Why?"

"I can do the Curly Shuffle," Hank said. "She went to Bennington. They don't teach that there."

I went into Susan's office and stood in front of her desk. She looked up from her computer screen when she saw me and smiled. "Have another story for me already?" she said.

"I've been invited to a Three Stooges luncheon," I said. "And they said I could bring someone."

Susan sat back in her chair, still holding the smile. "What exactly is a Three Stooges luncheon?"

"I'm not really sure," I said. "But I get made an honorary Stooge and meet some of the folks in the fan club."

"And you want me to go with you?"

"I figured since you were the editor who ran the piece," I said.

"There's no girlfriend you'd rather take?" she asked.

"I don't have a girlfriend," I said. "But once word gets out I'm an honorary Stooge, my dance card will be pretty full."

Susan looked at me for a moment and then nodded. "Okay," she said. "Just let me know the day and time."

"Great," I said. "You're going to have a fun time. I'll make sure of it."

"I'm not going to get hit with a pie, am I?" she asked as I started to make my way out of her office.

"I doubt it," I said. "But don't wear your best outfit, just in case."

THREE MONTHS AFTER the article ran, I was promoted out of movie timetables and into Susan's department. There was no increase in salary, but it was a much better job. I now had access to the story schedules and could better understand how the section was put together and the kind of stories Susan was most in need of. We worked closely every day, began going to screenings together in the evenings, and then took long walks or stopped at the Oyster Bar for a glass of wine to go over possible story ideas.

We were becoming friends, even though she knew very little about me and I knew less about her. I had heard she was from Cincinnati and her father was a doctor and her mother a nurse. I never asked about her personal life, but, based on the long hours she logged plus all the movies and plays she needed to attend, I couldn't imagine she had much time for one. Most days, she ate lunch at her desk, as did I. She read the New York dailies as well as some of the out-of-town papers as she ate.

She was quiet, classy, and reserved, and while a few of the reporters came around to ask her out, she always politely refused. The top editors of the paper thought her talented and respected her work ethic, though there was still the occasional sniping about her being a woman. Two senior members of the copy desk asked for transfers rather than work for a woman, but she shrugged off the snub and focused on the job she had to do.

I enjoyed working in her department and found her easy to talk to and even easier to make laugh. I was also learning by writing and observing how she edited a piece. She could turn a middling article into something stronger with a few subtle changes. I wrote for the section on a regular basis, choosing my stories based on what I knew and had absorbed growing up in Hell's Kitchen and the Bronx.

For example, I was a huge boxing fan, thanks in large part to my father. He had been a fighter in his youth and would bring home all the boxing magazines of the day, which I pored over as soon as he was done with them. He and his friends often told stories about the great boxers of the past, and I made sure to pay attention. So, when actor Tony Lo Bianco starred in a TV movie about the life of heavyweight champion Rocky Marciano, I was the first one in Susan's office pitching an essay on the legendary fighter. It ran for a full page and brought even more editors looking my way.

Then came my biggest breakthrough at the paper.

I wrote an article for the Sunday magazine about my mother. I wrote it without talking to anyone about it. I wanted it to be fun and entertaining, giving readers a glimpse into what it meant to grow up in a house where no one spoke English, Perry Como was worshipped, food and religion were the most discussed topics, and, no matter who an Italian mother's son married, she was never good enough.

When I finished the article, I brought it to Susan to get her input.

"This is the best thing you've written," she said, calling me into her office, the article clutched in her right hand. "It's warm, loving, and how much you care about your mom comes through in so many ways. You have fun with her, but you never make fun of her. That's an important distinction and one that can't be taught. You either know how to tread that line or you don't."

"They mean well," I said. "My mom and her friends really believe those crazy things they believe. And who knows? Maybe they're right."

"That's what I mean," Susan said. "You *get* them and can write about them in a way few can. That alone will take you a long way."

She showed me the few changes she had made to the piece, and I signed off on them. Then, together, we brought it in to the editor of the magazine, David Hershey. They both thought the piece was everything I wanted it to be, and Hershey asked if I would pose for the cover with my mother.

"I don't know about that," I said, caught by surprise. "My mom hates to leave the apartment and hates having her photo taken even more."

"This will be different," Hershey said. He was smart, savvy, a skilled editor with a razor-sharp sense of humor. "Other than the three and a half million people who buy the Sunday paper, no one will see her picture."

"If it helps any, I'll give her a call," Susan said.

"I wasn't kidding in the piece," I said. "My mom doesn't speak English. Not a word."

"I want to run it and I want to put it on the cover," Hershey said. "But I'll need photos. Your mom doesn't need to speak English to have her picture taken. You just need to get her here, have her bring a few changes of clothes, and we'll get it done down in the photo studio. Won't take more than a couple of hours, and I'll even make sure she gets a nice lunch out of it."

"My mom won't eat anything she hasn't cooked herself," I said.

"In that case," Hershey said, "have her bring enough food for all of us."

I WENT HOME and relayed the news to my mother and told her that the editor wanted to put us both on the cover of the Sunday magazine and she needed to come to the paper and have her photo taken.

"Why do they need to take my photo?" she asked.

"The story I wrote is about you," I said.

My mother stared at me for a few moments and then asked, "Does your story make fun of me?"

I shook my head. "There are funny parts to it," I said. "But I didn't make fun of you. I would never do that."

"If I do this, will it help you?" my mother asked. "Will you get more money or a promotion?"

"I don't know about that, Mom," I said. "But having a magazine cover story will get attention from a lot of the editors at the paper."

She thought about it for a few days, spoke to a few friends, and then, reluctantly, agreed to pick out a few dresses and come and do the photo shoot. "But before I go," she said, "I need to get a gift for the editor you're always talking about. The one who you work for?"

"That's very nice," I said. "But you don't need to get her any-thing."

"I'm going to call my sister in Florence and have her go buy her a nice sweater," my mother said. "Just tell me her size and I'll do the rest."

"You don't have to get her a sweater from Italy," I said. "We can pick one out at J. C. Penney."

"Leave it to me," my mother said. "The best sweaters come from Florence. Not J. C. Penney's."

Two weeks later, I walked my mother into Susan's office and introduced them. My mother handed her a large bag and asked me to translate for her. "She got you a gift," I said to Susan. "It's from Italy. My aunt picked it out. I took a guess on the size, but I think it should fit."

"That's so sweet," Susan said, taking the bag and removing the sweater. "She didn't need to do that."

"She wanted to thank you for everything you've done for me," I said.

Susan tried on the sweater and it fit perfectly. And my mother was right. Florence *did* have the best sweaters. Susan was genuinely moved by the gesture. She walked from behind her desk and went up to my mother and gave her a warm hug. "Thank you so much," she said. "It's beautiful."

My mother returned the hug and smiled at Susan, and it was a smile that stayed with her the rest of that afternoon.

For the first time in many years, my mother was the center of attention and was doted on by everyone who met her, and she loved every minute of it. I had never seen her so happy. On our way to the photo shoot, I introduced her to a friend who worked on the copy desk. He spoke Italian, and my mother asked him what he did at the paper.

"As little as possible," he said. "And they still pay me every week."

"Bravo," my mother said.

Looking back on it now, it was one of the best days of my mother's life.

A few months later, the piece ran, both of us featured on the cover of the *Daily News* Sunday magazine. The cover line read: MY ITALIAN MOM. It garnered quite a bit of attention and put me in position to be promoted to trainee reporter, working directly for Susan.

We worked closely together, but the relationship was still strictly a friendship. I was starting to feel, though, that what we had was heading in a more serious direction. At least for me. Away from work, I found myself constantly thinking about her. In a way, it was as if we were already dating—we would go out for drinks after a screening or a play; we would have long lunches at least twice a week—but most of the conversation revolved around work and story ideas. Occasionally, we drifted into more-personal topics, but even then, we never discussed our feelings for one another. I wasn't certain Susan felt the same about me as I did about her, but I had a strong feeling she did.

I was still very reluctant to tell her. I didn't want to do or say anything that would put our close friendship in jeopardy. Besides, there were so many hurdles in our way. Susan was seven years older than I was, and she was my boss, which would make a romantic relationship difficult. Especially at a paper that frowned on workplace romances.

There was also one other major obstacle to our developing a relationship: Susan had recently gotten married.

In the period between the writing of the article on my mom and its publication, one of her brothers introduced her to a divorced man from Cincinnati with two teenage children, and soon afterward they were married. It was a commuter marriage, Susan flying out every Friday evening to Ohio and returning late Sunday night. She barely spoke about her husband, and there was a visible sadness to her during those early weeks of the marriage. But everyone on her staff respected her privacy, and none of us asked any questions about her husband. During the workweek it was as if he didn't exist.

Susan liked to have lunch at a small, dingy pub next to Tudor City. The place reeked of greasy burgers, fries, and beer, and she loved going there. It was never crowded, and we would often have long lunches on Friday afternoons after the section had been closed and printed. She always ordered a bacon cheeseburger with fries and a glass of white wine.

"I couldn't sleep the other night, so I put *Gone with the Wind* in the VCR," she said to me during one of those lunches. "I stayed up until four in the morning watching it. Such a great movie."

"Had you seen it before?" I asked.

"Dozens of times," she said. "And I'll probably see it a dozen more."

"You know, up until a few years ago, I thought the music from the movie was the theme song for *Million Dollar Movie*," I said. "Never thought it was from an actual film."

"You've *never* seen *Gone with the Wind?*" she asked. "It's a classic. My second-all-time-favorite movie."

"No," I said. "It's never been up there with my must-sees. Wait, you said second-favorite. What's top of your list?"

"You'll laugh if I tell you," Susan said, smiling. "Maybe I should save that nugget until we get to know each other better."

"This *is* how people get to know each other better," I said. "You could tell a lot about a person based on the movies, shows, and books they like. So, go out on a limb and tell me."

"*Smokey and the Bandit,*" Susan said. "See, you may not be laughing, but I know you want to. You're just being polite."

"I'm not, really," I said. "I had a great time watching that movie. Burt Reynolds is the best, and Jackie Gleason can do no wrong in my book—from *The Honeymooners* to *The Hustler,* he's tough to beat."

"Now that we've exposed my movie tastes, let's have a look at yours," Susan said. "What are your favorites?"

"*Angels with Dirty Faces* ranks number one, by far," I said. "After that, probably *Casablanca* and *White Heat* in a toss-up tie."

"I've never heard of *Angels with Dirty Faces,*" Susan said.

"You're kidding," I said. "Then you're missing out on a great movie. It's got everything—Cagney, Bogart, O'Brien, the Dead End Kids, Sheridan, and an ending that will make you cry and give you something to argue over. Does Rocky Sullivan turn yellow before he goes to the electric chair, or did he do it for the kids? It's a question for the ages. I know every line of dialogue from that movie. Watch it every Christmas."

"How festive," Susan said. "While we're at it, you have favorite authors?"

"Alive or dead?" I asked.

"Both," Susan said.

"Alexandre Dumas is tops, with Victor Hugo and Rafael Sabatini a close second. Jack London, Arthur Conan Doyle, and Edgar Allan Poe round out the top tier. As for the living ones, I read everything by Harry Crews, Elmore Leonard, George V. Higgins. And, of course, Hamill and Breslin. Your turn."

"Trollope and Austen would be on the top of my list," Susan said, picking at the last of her fries. "And I think John Irving is the best novelist around right now."

"We really are from two different worlds," I said, laughing.

"Two different planets would be closer to the truth," she said.

"How about plays and musicals?" I said. "Do we dare head into that territory?"

"Any musical by Sondheim," Susan said. "And any drama by Edward Albee. Your turn."

"If it's Neil Simon or David Mamet, I'm there," I said. "And if Bob Fosse is doing a musical, you have to fight to keep me out of the theater."

"You do surprise me sometimes," she said. "I figured on Mamet and Simon. I didn't see Fosse coming."

"He does for musicals what Raymond Chandler did for mystery novels," I said. "Gets them out of that *Seven Brides for Seven Brothers* crap and makes them dark, sexy, and real."

"I love *Seven Brides for Seven Brothers*," she said.

"Why am I not surprised?" I said.

"We should get the check and head back," Susan said, signaling a passing waiter. "Unless you want to kick around favorite television shows."

"Now that you've mentioned it, I need to know," I said.

"Favorite TV show, all-time?" Susan said.

"Top of your list," I said. "The one you just have to see over and over and over again."

"*Star Trek,*" she said.

"Okay," I said. "You're right. We crossed into one dimension too many."

"And we didn't even get to poets," Susan said.

"Langston Hughes," I said. "Hands down."

"You got me again," Susan said, as we walked out of the restaurant. "Another one I didn't see coming."

"What can I say?" I asked. "I'm full of surprises."

"I'm starting to see that," Susan said.

1980–1988

❧

SUSAN'S MARRIAGE DISSOLVED in a matter of months and a quick divorce soon followed. The only time she mentioned anything about it to me was once at the end of an editorial meeting. The two of us were alone, scanning the wall calendar in her office, going over upcoming assignments. She put down her red felt-tip pen and lowered her head. "I wanted it to be perfect," she said. "And it wasn't anywhere close. It was a bad fit from the start. And, on top of it, he took all my money."

I stared at her for a moment, concerned, but at the same time not eager to pry into her private matters. "What do you mean he took your money?" I finally asked.

"He needed money for his businesses," she said. "So I gave him what I had. All that I had. Twenty-five thousand. And now it's gone."

"Did you ask him to pay you back?" I said.

"I wanted out, and trying to get my money back would have held up the divorce," she said.

I nodded and stayed silent, retraining my focus on the assignment calendar.

"I'm sorry," Susan said. "I shouldn't have said anything. I didn't mean to make you uncomfortable."

"And you didn't," I said. "I'm sorry you had to go through all that. A short marriage that didn't work, you can pretty much write off. But to lose all your savings on top of it, that would be tough for anybody."

"Would you have walked away?" Susan asked, tears forming at the corners of her eyes. "From the money, I mean. Not the marriage."

I hesitated before answering. "You did what you felt you had to do," I said. "And no one but you could have made that decision. I'm in a whole different place, so it wouldn't be fair to compare what you did to what I might have done."

"That means you wouldn't have walked away," Susan said, managing a slight smile. "You would have tried to get your money back."

"I would have more than tried," I said. "I would have ended up with either my money or a prison sentence. Either way, he would have been on the losing end of the situation."

I rested my right hand on her arm. "You need to move away from it," I said. "The next guy you fall in love with will be a lot better. Trust me."

"I hope that turns out to be true," Susan said, looking at me and resting a hand against mine.

"I know it will be," I said. "Without a doubt."

I REALIZED I was falling in love with Susan. She had a magical smile and a contagious laugh. She took her work seriously but never herself. She was kind, and hidden beneath her shyness was a warmth that couldn't be missed. I could listen to her talk all day and feel any worries I had dissolve, swept up by her sweet, low, and mellow voice. She had a great sense of humor and was razor-sharp smart. She was trim and sexy but never shied away from a Big Mac with a side of fries or a cold glass of cheap white wine. And she had the greatest legs in the world. Susan was the kind of woman men would go to battle over. And she was the kind of woman who could steal your heart and make you happy she did.

But despite my feelings, I didn't want to be a rebound guy. I needed it to be a real love affair and not merely a temporary bridge until the emotional wounds healed. I wasn't thinking about getting married or moving in together. But just dating would prove to have enormous implications. If I was assigned cover stories, for example, would it be because I was the best writer for that particular story or because I was going out with the boss? On a newspaper as competitive and often small-minded as the *News* was during those years, it would be a major hurdle for both of us to overcome.

And to top it off, I wasn't certain Susan felt the same way about me as I did about her. But I had a sense she was struggling with the same issues. I gave it a lot of thought, sitting by myself at the bar in Costello's, nursing a glass of red wine. I loved being in there, not just because it was the place the editors and reporters at the paper congregated after work but because of its history. In the dining room, one wall had been illustrated by the great cartoonists of the twentieth century—color drawings supplied by Bill Gallo, Al Capp, and so many others. The wall across from the bar was where James Thurber, on nights when he had more than his fill of drink, would crawl up on a stool and use a nail to carve sketches into the gray slate. Plus, the place took pride in having the worst waiters in New York City. And they loved playing to the *News* crowd. They were all from Ireland and treated anyone from the paper as if they were family members.

It was a drinking place from another time, another era, and every night you could hear reporters and editors regale the crowd with tales, whether true or exaggerated, about how a variety of stories were chased down across the years. It was a boisterous room of braggarts, prizewinners, and old-school newsmen, drinking and telling stories. For a young reporter, it was a graduate school class of storytelling, and I absorbed every tale, tall or not.

But as much as I enjoyed my nights in Costello's, I jumped at any chance to go to a screening with Susan or stop for a drink with her at a near-empty Oyster Bar. There, we would talk over possible story ideas for the next issue, or catch up on the latest office rumors, or discuss a book or television show one of us was currently obsessed with. We got to know each other during those nights and discovered there was more common ground between us than we had initially thought. Those were nights I never wanted to see end. But it had reached a point where I needed to know if we were friends or if there was something deeper at play.

I knew making the first move would be risky for me, but I felt I had to take that risk. It was the only way for me to find out her true feelings toward me. Were we merely good friends who worked together? Or did she feel about me as I had grown to feel about her, prevented from expressing herself because of her position as my boss and the age difference? Would she think me a young man who had simply developed a crush on a woman he worked for and shrug it off as a feeling that would pass over time? Would she be insulted at my crossing a line in a relationship she saw as a friendly one and decide to bring our Oyster Bar nights to an end?

I felt what was being left unspoken between us needed to be brought out into the open. If I allowed it to continue the way we were going and Susan did have feelings for me, then she would come to the conclusion that I didn't return them and would leave it at that. I had to make the leap and get an answer. Each time we said our goodbyes—Susan heading to her downtown apartment and me to mine in the East Bronx—I always lingered, standing in front of Grand Central, watching her walk toward Second Avenue in search of a cab, wanting more than anything to be by her side.

My slow walk back to the Metro-North platform for the thirty-minute train ride to the Wakefield station was always the loneliest and saddest part of an otherwise magical night.

* * *

IT WAS A hot and humid August night when I finally got up the nerve to broach the matter with Susan. There was no screening scheduled for that evening, no Broadway show she needed to see, the schedule light due to the time of year. The city was summertime quiet and empty, and anyone who wasn't away on vacation rushed to get out of the oppressive heat, heading home to a cool room and a cold drink.

We sat in our regular spot at the Oyster Bar, leaning against the cool leather, and ordered two glasses of white wine and some ice water. Despite the coolness of the bar, the back of my shirt was damp, and my rolled-up sleeves were wrinkled and wet to the touch.

"I can't wait for winter," Susan said, as the waiter quickly came back with our drinks. "And I *hate* winter."

I took a sip of wine and turned to look at her. "I need to tell you something," I said. "And ask you something. I'm just a little nervous about how exactly to do it. I'm not very good at this sort of thing."

Susan raised her glass and smiled. "The first time we spoke, you barged into my office to pitch a story about the Three Stooges," she said. "Despite your friends telling you I didn't like you and probably wouldn't give you the time of day. You weren't nervous then. You shouldn't be now."

"That was about a story I wanted to write," I said. "This is a lot different."

Susan reached out a hand and rested it on top of mine. "Tell me," she said.

I nodded and took a second sip of wine. "These last few months, getting to know you, going to screenings with you and ending our nights here, drinking wine, talking, telling stories, or just sitting quietly, have been the best weeks of my life," I said.

"It's been great for me, too," Susan said. "It's no secret I was pretty depressed a few months back. These nights spent with you helped me put that in the past."

"I'm not just talking about us becoming good friends," I said. "I mean, I'm happy that's happened, but I think it's gone deeper than that. At least for me. I'm in love with you, and I think you feel the same way about me. I hope I'm not wrong and I hope I'm not freaking you out right now. But I just need to know. I've never met anyone like you, and I certainly didn't think I would fall in love with someone like you. But, sitting here now, no matter how you feel about all this from your end, I'm glad I did. The time spent with you these past few months has been more than worth it."

Susan stayed quiet for several moments, her hand still gripping mine, tighter now. "I do feel the same about you," she said. "But I'm afraid. Not of falling in love with you. But what falling in love with you could mean for your career and mine."

"They'll gossip about us for a few weeks," I said. "We'll both be kidded about it. But, after a while, they'll move on. We wouldn't be the first ones working there to go out. We both can name people who met and married working there. Why would we be treated any differently?"

"Those other couples were reporters," Susan said. "I'm an editor and you work for me. That's not going to be greeted with hugs and smiles."

"Then we keep it quiet for a while," I said. "Look, we've been going out to screenings and the theater now for a few months, leaving the office together, not bothering to hide it. No one's raised any red flags. That's because they're not expecting someone like you to be going out with someone like me. It plays to our advantage."

"You should be dating someone your own age," Susan said. "I'm seven years older than you. It may not matter to you now, but one day it might."

"I'm not in love with someone my age," I said. "I'm in love with you."

"I wasn't kidding when I told you I thought you should be writing books and scripts," Susan said. "I really believe you have a great career ahead of you. One that will take you beyond this newspaper. I don't want to do anything to harm that."

"If that turns out to be true, that would be great," I said. "But if all I got to write were newspapers articles for the rest of my life, that would be great, too. What I'm going to end up doing or not doing is not what this is about. This is about us and what we're going to end up doing."

"What if it doesn't work out?" Susan asked. "In a few months you might feel differently about me than you do tonight. Even if no one at the paper suspects, a breakup would hurt our working relationship and might even bring an end to our friendship. I would hate to see either one of those two happen."

"Then let's make sure they don't," I said. "I know I'm younger than you, but that doesn't mean I'm walking into this with my eyes closed. I know what the risk factors are, and I've considered them all. And none of them have changed the way I feel. I love you, Susan."

Susan smiled, leaned over, and kissed me for the first time. "I love you, too," she whispered.

It was a perfect moment. A moment that, for me, has been frozen in memory for over forty years.

And it will stay with me until my last breath.

SOON AFTER THAT night, I moved in with Susan, sharing her studio apartment on East 15th Street. We kept a lid on our relationship for eighteen months. While we both enjoyed the secrecy and the privacy such an arrangement allowed, there were many awkward moments that came up as a result. There were only two people at the paper we trusted with our secret—Hank Gallo and Eddie Fay, both now working for Susan in her department. Neither one said a word to anyone about it and always helped buffer potential suitors who tried to step between Susan and me.

On a number of occasions, Susan was asked out to dinner by a reporter at the paper, and while she always declined politely, one or two wouldn't take no for an answer. That's where Eddie stepped in.

"What the hell is her problem?" one reporter asked him after a turndown. They were standing a few feet from Susan's office, speaking in hushed tones. "I'm single, she's single, and I only asked her out for a meal. She doesn't say yes to anyone."

"Maybe she's seeing someone," Eddie said.

"Then why not just say so?" the reporter said.

Eddie leaned in closer. "Maybe because, and this is just a guess, it's none of your business who she's seeing or who she's not," he said. "Maybe she's worried if the guy she is seeing finds out you asked her out, he might not like it and he might come looking to do something about it."

"Have you met this guy?"

"Again, none of your business who I met," Eddie said. "Just leave it alone. As far as you're concerned, she's off-limits."

By this time I was an entertainment reporter at the paper, writing, on average, three stories a week. While I enjoyed writing profiles of celebrities and theme pieces based on movies and television shows, my favorite part of the job was interviewing authors. I wrote pieces on Harold Robbins, Robin Cook, Irving Wallace, Robert Ludlum, James Clavell, and P. D. James, among many others. My time spent in their company, asking questions about their work, their process, the path that led them to being able to write books, served as an education for me. I soaked up the information they fed me and took it to heart. Each one left me with an indelible lesson.

Harold Robbins, at the time the most successful author in the world, was of special interest to me since he grew up in a Hell's Kitchen orphanage. The day before I was to interview the author, the book critic of the *News* ripped his new novel to shreds. As I sat across from Robbins, I saw the review clipped and resting by his elbow. "Do me a favor would you, kid?" he asked.

"If I can," I said.

"This critic from your paper, you know him?"

"We're not pals," I said. "But, yes, I know him."

Robbins reached into a bag resting on a chair and pulled out a large photo and handed it to me. "Give him this, would you?" he asked. "As a thank-you for his tearing my book a new hole."

It was a color photo of a boat, three levels high, taken at night, lit up like a casino. "That's my yacht," Robbins said. "Got it with the dough I made from the book he hated. He can hang it on the wall of whatever dump he lives in."

It was, I thought at the time, a perfect Hell's Kitchen move by a poor kid who clawed his way to the top of his profession.

INTERVIEWING BESTSELLING AUTHORS was one part of my writing education. Living with Susan was another.

She was a voracious reader and did not discriminate, moving easily from a Henry Fielding novel to a Jack Higgins thriller. She devoured magazines and newspapers and would clip articles she thought would be of interest to me. The weekends were our private time together. We would have breakfast and go through the morning papers, coming up with ideas for possible stories from the pieces we took note of. From there, we either went to a matinee of a play she thought I would enjoy or walked to the Upper East Side to get lost in a new museum exhibit or headed over to Chelsea to check out the large expanse of art galleries, looking at the many works on display.

I loved old movie posters and Sherlock Holmes memorabilia, and Susan knew a shop that specialized in both. During that first year together, Susan gave me a one-sheet from *Angels with Dirty Faces*, a kneeling and contrite James Cagney with Pat O'Brien, dressed in priestly garb, standing over his boyhood friend, praying for the "boy who couldn't run as fast as I could." It hangs framed to this day in my office.

Susan was a gifted editor and sharpened and honed the stories I wrote, making them read much better. We made each other laugh and we learned from one another. And she never doubted I would find success as a writer, not just at the *Daily News* but in places I had not even imagined.

Living in secret was a great deal of fun, but we were both eager to get married and start a family, and in early 1981 we decided to do just that. Before we told anyone at work about our decision, we spoke to our families. While we were both braced for some blowback, we never could have envisioned how much of a storm the notion of our marriage would cause.

Susan's parents thought it was a bad idea, citing the age difference as one of several key factors, adding a recent failed marriage and our working together into the mix of concerns. At least their argument seemed reasonable to me, fueled in part by the fact that her father was battling cancer and didn't need the additional worry about his only daughter marrying someone he thought was unsuitable.

My mother's reaction was filled with as much anger and venom as I'd heard from her in years. Susan was everything she didn't want for me in a wife—older, divorced, not Italian, and a smoker. She refused to come to the wedding and convinced my father not to go as well. My half brother and his wife also did not attend.

Susan and I held firm and dealt with each blow as it came and let nothing get in the way of our plans. "They don't want to come, that's their call," I said to Susan one night over dinner. "We go our own way and we make our own family."

"Will you regret it one day?" Susan asked. "Your parents not being there?"

"No," I said. "But I'll never forget it, either. My half brother, too. They've never been there for me when I've really needed them. Why should my wedding day be any different?"

Over the course of my life, I have forgiven my blood family for many things. This is one sting whose burn has never left me.

In their place, our friends and co-workers stepped up in the most unexpected and pleasant of ways.

One morning soon after we had made our decision public, the assistant managing editor of the paper, Jack Sanders, asked us both to come into his office. He was an excellent editor with a sly sense of humor and a warm manner. He had come to the *News* after a stint at *Newsweek* and, more impressive to me, had published four books. He sat behind his desk, a wide smile on his face and an unlit cigar jammed in his mouth. "I want to tell you how happy I am for you. Louise is, too. She claims she knew you two were together a few months back when we had you and some of the other reporters up at the house for a weekend barbecue. She could tell by the way you were looking at each other."

"That's one reason she might have known," I said.

"What's another?" Jack asked.

"I told her," I said.

Susan shook her head and smiled. "I did, too," she said.

Jack sat back and laughed. "Good thing you went into this business," he said. "You would have sucked as spies."

"Thanks, Jack," I said. "For everything you've done. For the both of us."

"You were the first editor to even bother speaking to me," Susan said. "If it weren't for you, I wouldn't have taken a job here. And if I hadn't, well, I suppose I would have never met 007 here."

"I have a favor to ask you two," Jack said. "And I can't go home if you say no."

"What is it?" I asked.

"Louise has always wanted a backyard wedding," Jack said. "We would love it if you got married at our house."

I nodded. "That would be great," I said. "But I think the final decision should be left to the bride-to-be."

Susan had her head lowered, and I could see tears welling in her eyes. "Thank you," she said in a low voice. "That would make that day very special for us." The tears shed were not ones of sadness but of joy, freeing her from the negative reaction of our families and allowing her to fully embrace the happiness of those who were truly closest to us.

Susan and I were married on a warm mid-May afternoon in 1981 in the small Westchester County town of Pound Ridge. We were surrounded by fifty guests, a reverend whose name we never knew, and twenty-five Neapolitan mastiffs, since Louise bred them and kept them around her five-acre property. Susan looked radiant, the dogs were well behaved, and we danced, drank, and sang well into the morning hours. It was a wedding like no other and a day that is firmly and happily etched in my memory.

It was a potluck wedding, with a number of the guests given key assignments—from choosing the music to setting up transportation from the city to making sure there was enough food and drink.

And while we didn't write our own vows, Susan did alter them slightly.

A few nights before the wedding, she was reading over the vows, a pencil curled in her right hand. "You going to edit the vows?" I asked, smiling at her.

"Just making one small change," she said. "I have no problem with love and honor, but obey has got to go. Wrong word. Wrong century."

"The same holds true for me, then, right?" I asked.

"Yes," Susan said, crossing out the word and smiling back at me. "But I'm not worried. You usually do what I ask you to do anyway."

LESS THAN A year into our marriage, Susan became pregnant with our first child, a daughter we would name Kate. Susan's schedule called for her to work later hours than mine, since she needed to edit the stories and stay until the pages were locked in. This did not prevent her from signing us both up for a number of classes, from birthing to first-aid courses at the American Red Cross. "If I can't make any of them," she said to me as I was looking over the class schedules, "you go and take notes. It'll be fun. You'll make friends. You'll see."

Susan made it to one class.

The rest of the six-week course, I was paired up with a petite British woman whose husband worked long hours on Wall Street. Over the course of the classes, we got to know each other pretty well. I like to think, even all these years later, that despite my absence at the actual event, the lessons she and I shared helped her make it through to a successful delivery.

Kate arrived two weeks ahead of schedule.

It was a warm late morning in March and I was sitting in the front seat of a yellow cab, Susan and two of her friends crammed in the back. We were heading to Lord & Taylor for a big sale, and I wasn't quite sure why I was dragged along, other than to help carry the many items they were planning to buy.

Halfway through the trip, Susan suddenly sat up and said, "We need to get to the hospital. Now."

I turned around and stared at her and she nodded at me. "I think my water broke."

I looked at the cab driver. He was a middle-aged man with a kind face. Up until that moment we had been talking about the upcoming baseball season and how much we missed watching the games. "Forget Lord & Taylor," I said. "We need to get to Mount Sinai as fast as you can."

"Don't worry, kid," the man said. "This ain't the first time I've had to make a hospital run."

"Run the lights if you have to," I said. "I'll pay for any tickets you get."

He made a sharp U-turn, ignored the honking horns coming at us from all sides, and drove as if we were in the middle of a high-speed chase. We came to a sudden stop in front of Mount Sinai. One of Susan's friends ran in to get a nurse and a wheelchair. I emptied my pockets and gave the driver all the money I had. "You did a great job," I said. "Thank you."

"Kiss the baby for me," he said with a smile.

Susan was rushed up to the maternity wing, and I went to the front desk to let them know we were there and to make sure the paperwork Susan had filled out weeks earlier was accurate. After a few moments of searching, asking me to spell and respell my name, a woman behind a thick counter told me, "Can't find anything under either name. But no worries. We can start from scratch. Won't take more than ten minutes, if that."

Susan's friend Carol came up next to me. "They can't find the paperwork," I told her. "We have to do it over again."

The woman sat behind a typewriter and without raising her head asked, "Mother's name?"

By this time, all I could think about was Susan on a gurney in a delivery room, wondering where the hell I was. "Her mother's name," I said. "Her mother's name is Helen."

The woman typed and then asked, "Mother's age?"

"I don't know," I said. "She's sixty-eight maybe, sixty-nine. Around that."

Carol reached over and rested a hand on my arm. "Give me your medical cards," she said in a low soft voice. "I'll do the rest. You go up and find Susan."

Susan was in labor for four and one-half hours. I was by her side the entire time, though in looking back, I doubt I was very much of a help. I did my best to comfort her, but without much success. At one point in that stretch, the nurse assisting Susan's obstetrician, Dr. Sher, looked at both of us and said, "There's some blood there."

"She's bleeding?" I asked.

"Not your wife," the nurse said. "You're the one bleeding. She cut your hand."

Susan had gripped my hand so tightly that her nails dug around my forefinger and thumb, breaking the skin and cutting into the area. I asked the nurse, "Do you have anything for my cut?"

Susan looked at me and said, "Are you kidding? You're asking for medical attention?"

"It's not going to take her too long," I said. "Peroxide and a Band-Aid and I'll be good to go."

None of the lessons I learned in the classes I had taken with my British partner had any effect on Susan. At one point during the delivery, I said, "I had my bag all packed. I just didn't think it would happen this early. I even bought the tennis balls."

Susan was a mask of pain and sweat. "And why would you need to bring a tennis ball?" she managed to ask.

"To rub it along your back," I said. "It's supposed to make you feel better. The lady I was partnered with seemed to like it."

"Then go find her and rub the tennis ball on her back," Susan said. "And when you're done, you know what you can do with it."

Then, as if out of a dream, it all came to a beautiful ending. At 3:57 P.M. on a Friday afternoon, I was handed a small set of clippers by the doctor and asked to cut the cord on our newborn daughter. I did and then stood back as the baby was cleaned by a nurse and handed to Susan to hold. Standing there, watching the two of them together, remains one of the most memorable moments of my life.

WITH A NEWBORN and both of us working at a paper facing financial difficulties, the time had come for me to look for another job. After a few months, I made the move, landing at Time Inc. for a new start-up magazine, *TV-Cable Week*. The night before I accepted the position, Susan and I went for a long walk, me pushing Kate in her carriage. "You think it's the right thing to do?" I asked her. "I know it's more money and better benefits, but it's a start-up, and some of those make it and some don't."

"You've learned as much as you could from working at the paper," Susan said. "It's going to be a great experience, no matter how long it lasts. You'll be working with a higher caliber of editors, who'll push you to write better and approach a story from an angle you haven't even thought about. It's a risky move but a smart one. Your work has suffered since they moved you to city-side. Every story ends the same—he said, she said, or according to. That's not writing. That's typing."

"I don't have you editing my pieces," I said. "I send them to my editor, and they run as I wrote them. Some days I wonder if he even reads them."

"They hard-edit at Time Inc.," Susan said. "The editors are all former writers, and excellent ones at that. It's the best place for a young writer."

"But you'll still be my favorite editor," I said, smiling. "I don't care how good this new crew turns out."

"I'll be there when you start writing books," Susan said. "I'll be your first read once you work on those."

"Since we met, you have this vision of me writing books," I said. "Why are you so convinced I can even write a book, let alone get someone to pay me to do it?"

"You have stories to tell," Susan said. "You come from a world, a life, that so many can relate to, and the people you know don't get written about often. Do I think you're going to write a book about a New England professor who has an affair with one of his students and is blocked on a novel? No. You would be terrible at that. It's not your world."

I reached over and put an arm around her shoulders, pushing Kate's carriage with one hand. "What is my world?" I asked.

"Criminals, cops, honest working people, Italians, people who leave for work before the sun comes up and come back home when it's down," she said. "You had a father in prison for killing his wife. You spent summers on a beautiful island in Italy. I know you think you're not well educated."

"I don't just think it," I said. "When you and your Bennington friends sit around and talk books, more than half the time I don't know who the hell you're talking about. The gaps in my education are canyon wide."

"Those blanks are easy to fill in," Susan said. "You can pick up those lessons in a library. But what you've learned can't be taught. I can empathize with the stories you've told me about your life, but I come away from hearing them wondering if I could have survived them."

"From what you told me about growing up with your parents, it didn't sound like Disney World," I said. "It was harsh and cruel."

"In many ways it was," Susan said. "But in my case, it was emotional cruelty. It was never physically abusive. You go to therapy for the emotional part. I don't know where you go to clear away memories of physical abuse. I like to think writing about it is one way to confront it."

"So basically you're saying I'm the Proust of Hell's Kitchen," I said. "I get that right?"

Susan laughed and rested her head against my shoulder. "Not even close," she said.

SUSAN WAS RIGHT about my year at Time Inc. The start-up magazine allowed me to learn from a group of talented writers and editors, among them Graydon Carter, of *Vanity Fair* fame, and Jonathan Black, who went on to run *Playboy* for a number of years. My writing improved as I learned the Time Inc. way of cramming as much information into a paragraph as possible while still keeping the piece in my own voice. It was a finishing school, and I soaked up as much as I could. But I was correct that the move came with a risk, and the start-up folded nine months after my first day.

That pit stop led to a four-year odyssey of moving from temporary work at established magazines to longer runs at start-ups. I did a three-month stint at *People* and spent six horrible months at *Crain's New York Business* and then a year at another start-up, *Entertainment Tonight* magazine, working for the legendary Harriet Fier.

The frustration of not knowing where I would be and for how

long wore on me. I wasn't able to crack through to the major magazines, writing for monthlies that no one would want to be caught reading in public.

In the midst of this, in 1986, Susan and I had our second child, a son, Nick.

This birth went off at warp speed. We had just finished dinner and were getting ready for bed when Susan clutched her stomach and we both sprang into action—calling a friend to stay with Kate, grabbing what we needed for the hospital, and phoning the doctor's office to let them know we were on our way.

Susan was wheeled into the delivery room a few minutes before midnight. A young doctor I had not met before came in and introduced herself and then checked out Susan and took a quick glance at the overhead clock. "This baby will be born in time for me to make it home to catch David Letterman," she said with a smile.

Back then, Letterman aired at 12:30 A.M., giving her less than thirty minutes to deliver our son. "Is there someone special on you really want to see?" I asked, slightly concerned about working against the clock.

The doctor shook her head. "Don't remember who's on tonight," she said. "Doesn't matter, though. Watching him helps me relax after a long day and get a good night's rest."

There was no time to give Susan an epidural and she was in agonizing pain, her loud screams echoing off the thick delivery room walls. "Do me a quick favor?" the doctor asked.

At this point I was afraid she was going to ask me to leave the room and find a television so she could watch David Letterman in the event Nick was born a few minutes into his opening monologue. "What do you need me to do?"

"I want you to clamp your hand tight across your wife's mouth," the doctor said. "Strong enough to keep her from screaming. That will force her to push down harder. All I need from her is one more solid push and we're home free."

I looked down at Susan and smiled. "This is the first and only time I'll have a chance to do this," I said.

I rested the palm of my right hand across Susan's mouth and held it there for less than a minute. Then, at 12:24 A.M., six minutes before the start of *Late Night with David Letterman,* our Nick was born.

A YEAR LATER, Susan left the paper and moved to *People* magazine, working for Jim Gaines. And in no time at all, under the guidance of the gifted Gaines, she shot up the masthead like a rocket—from senior writer to senior editor to assistant managing editor. It seemed to happen in no time at all.

I was proud of her rapid rise but depressed over it at the same time.

Not about her success. But at the gnawing feeling that I was merely riding her coattails. While she was the rising star at a major magazine, I was the lagging spouse moving from job to job and never writing anything worth reading. I didn't want to do anything to hurt her career or cause her embarrassment. It was a dark time for me, and I did my best to keep it from Susan, knowing she had more than enough to deal with, holding down a demanding job and helping to care for and raise two small children.

My job prospects were dwindling and I was wearying of the freelance life when another Time Inc. start-up offered me a position as a staff writer. The magazine was called *Picture Week,* and there really wasn't much writing of note to be done. It was a photo-driven publication, and most of the stories ran no longer than fifteen lines in length. It was boring, tedious work, and I dreaded every day I worked there. My only solace was that Harriet Fier had also joined the staff and seemed as unhappy as I was.

"I don't know how much longer I can do this," she said to me one day over lunch. "Working long hours to put out stories no one reads."

"I was here until four in the morning the other night, writing a twelve-line story to go with a full-page photo of a sea turtle," I said. "My editor bounced it back three times. He said I wasn't giving the story the attention it deserved. Twelve lines, written three different times, and then completely rewritten by him. And all anyone's going to do is look at a picture of the sea turtle and turn the page."

"Then why are you here?" Harriet asked.

"I got two kids and I need the money," I said. "What about you?"

"I'm turning my back to this first chance I get. And you should, too. Imagine having to do this for another twenty years, moving from job to job, one magazine to another. You'll end up bitter and angry, like most of the ones working here."

"I'm already bitter and angry," I said.

"Then get out," Harriet said. "After this one folds—and trust me, it will fold—find another way to make your way."

The magazine ceased publication a few weeks after that lunch, and once again I was out of work, facing an uncertain future and frozen in place, tired of the grind of the past few years, frightened about what the future held for me.

I SAT ACROSS from Susan at our dining room table. I poured her a fresh glass of white wine and reached for her hand. "I have to get a job," I said. "But not on a magazine. I'm done with that."

"So where will you look for work?" Susan asked.

"Anywhere," I said. "My father used to work down in the meat market, and they're always looking for people. Money's good, solid benefits. Or a department store. Or sell cars. I don't really care what I do. I just can't keep doing what I've been doing the last few years.

It's killing me on the inside and, if I keep doing it, it's going to make you sorry you ever met me, let alone married me."

"I know it's been tough," she said. "But you shouldn't quit. You should write. Not for the magazines. If you're ever going to be the writer I always believed you would be, now is the time to start. It's time to tell your stories."

"I'm the last writer on any editor's mind right now," I said. "I'm barely making enough to help keep up with the bills. Now you want me to write my stories. And what if I write them and no one wants to buy them? I know you think I should be writing books, but maybe that's not meant to be. Maybe you just think that because you love me."

"I don't *think* that," Susan said. "I *know* that. If you take the time to write a story, one that only you know and only you can write, somebody will want it. Put your heart into it and you'll see. People will want to read it."

"And if no one does?" I asked. "What then?"

"If that happens, and you want to quit and go on to something else, I won't stand in your way," Susan said. "But we'll both know you at least gave it a shot."

I let go of her hand and sat back in my chair. We sat in silence for several moments. "Where should I start?" I asked.

"There's only one place," Susan said. "It's time to write about your father."

1988 – 2012

❧

THE NEXT MORNING, I began to write the story that changed my life.

I wrote about my father and discovering at the age of fourteen that he had murdered his first wife and was convicted of second-degree manslaughter. It took less than a week to write the twenty-five-page article, and when I was finished, I left it on Susan's side of the bed for her to read when she got home from work.

I was no longer worried about an editor liking what I had written. But I desperately needed Susan's stamp of approval. Anything that might happen after that would be nothing more than vindication of her belief in my ability.

Susan came out of the bedroom holding the piece in her right hand. She had tears in her eyes and a smile on her face. "I can't just call it good," she said. "It's sad, painful, heartfelt, and powerful. I didn't change a word. There was no need. It's all there on the page."

We embraced and held on to each other for the longest time, rocking back and forth in silence. All the frustration I had felt for the past few years flowed out of me, replaced by a confidence I didn't know I could possess. And it had been put there by my wife, a petite, brown-haired, brown-eyed woman with an easy smile, whose belief in me never once wavered.

We sat on the couch and Susan rested the article on the coffee table. "So, what now, boss?" I asked, smiling. "Now that it's written, who should I send it to?"

"I'll take it to the office tomorrow," Susan said. "I'll show it to Jim Gaines. He's starting up a magazine called *Family Life,* and this might be just what he's looking for."

The next few months felt like days.

My life moved from struggling writer with no future to a string of offers flowing my way at a rapid pace. As a friend of mine said during that time, "You went from a guy who couldn't hit minor-league pitches to hitting the game-winning home run in the seventh game of the World Series in the blink of an eye."

Susan was right about Jim Gaines. He loved the article and handed it to two of his trusted deputies, Jay Lovinger and Peter Bonventre. They bought the piece for $7,500. The magazine Gaines was hoping to launch, *Family Life,* didn't get a go-ahead, so Lovinger took it with him when he became editor of *Life* magazine. It would be the longest article the magazine had ever run.

Around the same time, Keith Bellows, an editor working for Whittle Communications, offered me a three-month job putting together a one-theme issue of their *Special Reports* magazine. The job paid $50,000, and I would get an additional $5,000 to write the cover story. I hadn't made that much money in the prior two years, let alone in three months. At the time, Susan and I were buried under an avalanche of credit-card bills and other mounting debts, and neither one of us thought we would get out from under them.

"I read an interview with Jackie Gleason a few years back," Susan said over dinner the night after I agreed to the Whittle offer. "He said even if you are the unluckiest guy in the world, there comes a moment when that changes and the door to good luck opens just a crack. Once that happens, you have to be ready to make your move, because that door only stays open for a short time. And when it slams closed again, it stays closed for good."

"And you think this is the door opening for me now?"

Susan nodded. "And I think it's going to stay open for a bit longer," she said. "This is finally time to make your move."

"It's only a three-month deal," I said. "I'm grateful for it. But let's not get ahead of ourselves. I can be back scratching for work when this is over."

"No," Susan said. "You'll look back on this assignment and see it for what it was—the first step to becoming what I've always believed you could be."

I smiled at her and rested a hand on her cheek. "There had to have been doubts along the way," I said. "You always seem so confident about what I can do. Not even these past few years, when I was barely getting by, you never stopped believing it would get better. I questioned it every single day. At some point you must have thought you were wrong about me. That I was never meant to be anything more than a guy trying to make it to the end of the week."

"Not for one minute," Susan said. "I believed it when I read your first piece and I believed it even more every day since. But, to be totally honest, I didn't think it would take this damn long for you to make your move."

AS I WAS wrapping up work on the special issue, which focused on cops who found second careers in Hollywood, I got a call from an ex-cop turned TV producer I'd known for many years.

Sonny Grosso was one of the two detectives who broke the famous French Connection case that became the basis for the 1971 Academy Award–winning movie. He had been a technical adviser on a number of movies and television shows before branching out on his own.

He offered me a job on a syndicated talk show, which, in turn, led to a five-year stint working for him on *Top Cops*, a CBS series.

No one was happier about all this than Susan. We were both putting in long hours on the job, but we always made sure to be there for our two children. I took Nick with me to the office whenever he was off from school, and Grosso embraced him as if he were one of his own. And Susan did the same with Kate. We took them to movies, the theater, ball games, trips to visit my relatives in Italy.

That first trip back to Ischia was a memorable one. Susan and our kids got to see my real family, the ones who had embraced and loved me for many a summer. I took Susan, Kate, and Nick all over the island, visiting my favorite beaches and stopping at the Bar Calise to eat gelato, laughing and dancing along with the singer, who entertained us late into the night. They got to meet their cousins, aunts, uncles, and my many friends. But the most important part of our stay was that it gave me the chance to let them get to know Nonna Maria. I took them to her house and showed them where I had stayed and pointed to the photo of my Uncle John and told them his story. I walked with them up the hill and we sat on the stone bench, the one I had shared with Nonna Maria for many nights, and I told them as many stories about her as I could remember. Despite the years, Nonna Maria had never left me, and now she was a part of their lives, as well. Telling those stories and remembering my time with her was both the happiest part of the trip for me and the saddest.

THE NEXT LIGHTNING bolt of good fortune landed while I was putting together the staff for *Top Cops*. I had signed with a literary agent, and she sent the article I had written about my father to six publishing houses. The first week, we got three rejections. The second week, we had a six-figure sale to the publishing house I had always wanted to be published by—Random House.

And this is when life, as it so often does, gets in the way and brings with it a heavy dose of bad news to collide with the good. This has been the pattern throughout my life, and I have now learned to steel myself for the arrival of bad news.

I got the call from my agent at eleven in the morning, while I was at the *Top Cops* production office. The deal was done. I had sold my first book. I hung up the phone and immediately dialed Susan's office at *People* magazine. Her secretary said she was out but would be back in an hour. Told me she had a doctor's appointment. I asked that she call me soon as she got in. For that next hour, I closed the door to my office, sat back in my chair, and took in the moment. It had been a long time coming, and I couldn't wait to share the news with Susan. Because this wasn't just my moment. This was *our* moment. And, finally, after many years of struggle and rejection, this was now *our* time.

Susan called a few minutes past noon. "I need to tell you something," she said, her voice more subdued than usual.

"I have something to tell you, too," I said. "But go ahead, you first."

"I just got back from the eye doctor," Susan said. "I've had blurry vision in my right eye for a couple of days. I thought I had gotten some eye liner in it and that it would eventually clear up."

"Is that what the doctor thought it was?" I asked, shifting quickly from confident to concerned.

"No," she said. "It wasn't caused by eye liner."

"What is it?"

"I have a tumor on my optic nerve," Susan said. "And I need surgery. As soon as possible."

I sat back and nearly dropped the phone. I didn't say anything for several moments and neither did Susan, both of us allowing the weight of what she'd just said to sink in. "Will he be doing the surgery?" I managed to ask.

"It's a very delicate procedure," Susan said. "He's done about six in the past few years and he's willing to do it."

"But he doesn't think he should," I said.

"No, he doesn't," Susan said.

"If not him, then who?"

"The doctor who taught him the procedure," Susan said. "He does six a day. He's supposed to be the best in the country at this type of surgery. He's in Pittsburgh. Allegheny General Hospital."

"Then that's where we go," I said.

"We'll talk about it tonight," Susan said. "There's the kids to think of. If we go to Pittsburgh, we would need to be away for a week, if not longer. The sitter can't stay overnight, and we can't just leave them. They'll be scared enough as it is."

"We'll figure it out," I said. "You can't risk not going to the best doctor for the surgery."

"I should have waited to tell you," Susan said. "I shouldn't have told you while you were at work."

"Don't worry about work," I said. "Want me to come get you and take you home? Should you even be in your office?"

Susan chuckled. "Don't start worrying now," she said. "I'm fine. I'll wrap up a few things here and then head home. See the kids and make dinner."

"I won't be late," I said. "Just need to make two quick calls and then I'm out of here."

"You called earlier," Susan said. "Told Pauline you had something you needed to tell me."

"It's nothing," I said. "Just wanted you to know the pilot is coming together pretty well."

"Well, at least there's some good news for today," Susan said. "See you at home."

I walked from the *Top Cops* production office to our West Side apartment. I was lost in thought, realizing how quickly a good moment we both had worked years to achieve could dissolve in seconds, rendering it, at least for the time being, completely meaningless. My mind was no longer focused on a new TV series or a book I had just agreed to write. Instead, all that lay in front of me was the dread of the word "tumor" and all the horror that came with it.

Up until that day, I had thought of Susan as unstoppable. I was the hypochondriac, always running to the doctor with one perceived illness or another. She was the doctor's daughter, who never panicked when one of the kids got hurt or was ill, who knew exactly what to do, who was always calm and always in control.

And now my wife had a tumor, and I needed to step up and be there for her as she always had been for me.

I had never been as frightened of anything in my life as I was on that long, slow walk home. Without Susan by my side, none of what happened to me would matter as much. No success, no achievement, would compensate for her loss. From the day we moved in together, I never contemplated my life without her in it. Now, for the very first time, I saw that as a real possibility, and it was all I could do to keep one foot in front of the other.

THAT NIGHT, I helped Susan put the kids to bed and then we went to the living room and sat on the couch. I poured us each a glass of wine. She smiled at me and reached for my hand and held it. "Did you call your doctor back?" I asked. "To let him know you were thinking of having the surgery done in Pittsburgh?"

"I'll get to that tomorrow," Susan said. "I don't want to talk about it or even think about it tonight. Let's talk about something else. Get my mind off it."

I nodded. "I heard from my book agent today," I said. "She called early this morning."

"And?" Susan said in an excited voice. "What did she say? Did she hear from one of the other publishers?"

"Yes," I said. "Peter Gethers called her. He's an editor and the publisher of Villard. It's a Random House division."

"And what did he say?" Susan said. "Come on. Don't turn shy on me now. If there's ever a day I could use some good news, it's today."

"He's buying the book," I said. "He called me after I spoke to my agent and had agreed to his offer."

Susan rested her glass on the coffee table, reached out, and held me in her arms. "You did it," she whispered in my ear. "You really did it. Just like I knew you would."

I held her tighter, tears flowing down the sides of my face. "No," I managed to say. "I didn't do it. *We* did it."

IN THE END, thanks to the help of three close friends, my pal Hank among them, we made arrangements for Susan to have the surgery she needed in Pittsburgh. Saying goodbye to Kate, who was eight at the time, and Nick, not even four yet, was heartbreaking for her to do and for me to witness. Susan was silent during the short flight to Pittsburgh, not knowing if she would survive the delicate surgery or, if she did, in what kind of shape she would come out of it. The editors at her magazine and my boss on the television show couldn't have been more supportive. A few days before we left, I went to see Sonny and asked him to put someone else in charge of the show. "I know how important this series is to your company," I told him. "And I don't know how long it's going to take Susan to recover or even if she will recover. You should think of replacing me."

"First of all, you've both done everything you could," Sonny said. "You found the number-one guy in the country to do the surgery. And, as far as replacing you, that's not going to happen. This is life and death you're both facing. This other thing, it's just a television show. It's not my first and it won't be my last. Go do what you need to do."

All of Susan's anxiety and fears evaporated soon as we met with the surgeon. Dr. Joseph Maroon was wiry, handsome, and as confident as anyone considered the best in his field should be. He sat across from Susan, holding a skull in his right hand and with his left showing her the path he needed to take in order to remove her tumor. If at any point in his journey he grazed even one of the multiple nerve endings, it could blind her, leave her with an eyeball she could not control, or worse. There was also one additional factor he needed to inform her about. "I can't tell from the MRI if the tumor is resting on top of the optic nerve or if it's wrapped around it," he said. "If it's resting, that's a better scenario. If it's wrapped around the nerve, it's a problem."

He then put the skull down and looked at Susan and smiled. "That's the bad news," he said.

"Is there good news?" Susan asked. "If there is, I would love to hear it."

The surgeon nodded. "The good news is, you came to me," he said. "So, don't worry about anything. I'll take care of it."

He stood up, rested a hand on top of hers, and gave her a comforting wink. "I'll see you in surgery," he said.

SUSAN'S SURGERY WAS set the day after the first episode of *Top Cops* was to air on CBS. Late that afternoon, I went down the hall to get a cup of coffee, and as I walked back toward Susan's room, four nurses on the floor each told me how much they were looking forward to seeing the show that night. I nodded and smiled and went into Susan's room and sat on a leather chair across from her bed. Susan caught a look in my eye and asked, "What is it?"

"Nothing," I said. "It's just weird. On my way back, a bunch of nurses told me they couldn't wait to see the show tonight. I didn't think *anybody* but us knew it was going to be on."

"I wonder how they all knew?" Susan said. "Especially since they work the four-to-midnight shift and probably never get to see any television at all."

I looked at Susan and nodded. "You passed the word," I said.

"Somebody had to," Susan said.

"If nothing else, we'll get good numbers in Pittsburgh," I said.

Susan stayed silent for a few moments, lost in her own thoughts. "I need to talk to you, and I want to do it before they put any drugs in me," she said.

I rested my coffee container on top of a heating unit and stood next to her. "You feeling okay?" I asked. "You want me to call a nurse?"

"It's not about me," Susan said, her voice calm, controlled. "It's about you."

"What is it?"

"I don't want you to stop now," Susan said. "No matter what happens to me, you don't stop. This show, your first book, that's just the beginning. You're on your way, and I want you to keep going. Promise me you will. I need to hear it from you before I go into surgery."

"I don't know if I can promise that," I said. "What little I've done so far would not have happened without you. You pushed me, made me want to be better, kept me from quitting. It was more you than me."

"That's nice to hear," Susan said. "I did what I could to help you along. But now you have to keep it going. For me. And for the kids. It doesn't matter whether you want to do it or not. You have to. For all of us."

"You're going to make it through this," I said. "So let's stop this kind of talk. I can't think of you not being there with me. And I don't want to."

"Promise me," Susan said, squeezing my hand. "Please. Just promise me you will keep going no matter what happens."

I looked at her and nodded. "I promise," I said. "No matter what happens, I'll keep going, wherever this path leads. I won't let you down."

"You never have," Susan said.

She rested her head against a pillow and closed her eyes. I walked away from the bed and stared out the window, looking at a baseball field across the way from the hospital. Both of us lost to a swirl of thoughts too frightening to put into words.

SUSAN MADE IT through that surgery thanks to the skill of one of the best doctors in the world. While she would retain only 5 percent of the vision in her right eye, there were no complications and, after a few months, no scar. All that remained was the memory of that eventful week in Pittsburgh.

We both resumed our careers and kept them on an upward trajectory. Susan continued her rise at the magazine, and I moved from one book to another and also started to write scripts for movies and television. One of my books was made into a feature film, and we had enough money to pay off our debts and move out of the city to a house in Westchester County.

Kate and Nick went to the best schools they could get accepted to and started on career paths of their own. We traveled to Italy as much as possible, often on assignment for the *National Geographic Traveler*, edited by my friend from Whittle Communications, Keith Bellows. As always, on those assignments, Susan and I worked as a team—she did the digging and reporting, finding pieces of interest wherever we went, and I dutifully followed and then came home and wrote the articles.

They were the best times of our lives, and though it felt as if those days would never come to an end, I knew that we would eventually hit a bump in the road. I just never imagined it would be one that would shatter the world we had so lovingly and carefully constructed.

We did enjoy the ride, make no mistake about that. I got to work with editors, directors, writers, and producers I had for many years only read about. I was paid more money than I ever dreamed of earning. Susan was, for a few years at least, the golden editor of Time Inc., running special issues, from Princess Diana to Audrey Hepburn to a magazine devoted to weddings, which sold millions of copies.

Even Kate and Nick got involved in the family business. Nick was a pro-wrestling fanatic as a boy, and he adored the Rock. He hounded Susan to put the then-wrestler in one of her special issues— "The 50 Most Beautiful." She fought him off as best she could, but Nick, even at a young age, could make his case better than a courthouse lawyer, and Susan knew a good idea when she heard one.

Kate was part of the first Take Your Daughter to Work Day celebration and ended up on a segment of an ABC news program, talking about the day she spent working alongside her mother. Kate was also an excellent writer and had pieces published in several magazines, including *Time,* while she was still in high school.

But a crash always follows a high. We had a wonderful run, and then it began to unravel. First, Susan's career took a few unexpected and unhappy hits. She left *People* when it was clear she would not land the post of top editor. And from there began a frustrating trek from one magazine to another. Some of the stops were enjoyable— her three-year stint running a Hearst magazine, *Quick & Simple,* was the happiest I'd ever seen her at work. She loved the staff she put together and was proud of the magazine they put out each month. Prior to that was a dreadful time spent editing *Rosie,* a magazine named after the comedienne Rosie O'Donnell, which ended in a bizarre courtroom trial. She spent less than seven weeks at the helm of *OK!* magazine before she and the rest of the top staff were let go. In between, there were a handful of start-ups she edited that never made it past the development stages. She was fortunate to end her career run on a happy note, working for a few years as a senior editor at *More* magazine.

Despite these ups and downs, Susan kept her head up and continued to do what she did best—assign and edit stories, always staying true to the readers of the publications she served.

But the shift in her fortunes, the hectic roller-coaster turbulence of moving from one magazine to another, wore her down. There was no longer a track to her career. She experienced doubt practically on a daily basis and had lost some of her confidence. She hid it well from most of her friends and from our children, but the weight of the sadness she felt was difficult for me to ignore.

I was going through my own career crisis. I was still writing and publishing books; they just weren't selling as well as the earlier ones had. I was getting script offers, but they were coming in further and further apart. I was still earning a great living, but the money wasn't what it once had been. I hadn't become the bestselling author I'm certain my publisher envisioned after my initial success.

Susan also had to fight off a number of illnesses during this time. She had a minor brush with breast and thyroid cancer and suffered through a few serious bouts of stomach pains.

This period also led to the first major crack in our marriage.

We were both angry at our circumstances, and there was no one to vent it at other than each other. We had moved out of a house I loved back into Manhattan, to an apartment in Chelsea I didn't want to live in. "You grew up in Ohio, in a house with your own room and a pool," I once said to her during one of many arguments over the issue of moving. "Your dream was always to come live in the city. That wasn't my dream. I couldn't wait to get out of the city, and I never thought we would ever sell a house you knew I loved as much as I did."

"I never wanted a suburban life," Susan said. "I always wanted to come back. You should have known that."

"How could I have known that?" I asked. "You never said anything to me about it. And by the time you got around to telling me, your mind was already made up."

Looking back now, it was a frivolous argument. We had been together for over thirty years and, for the first time, a seed of mistrust had been planted between us. For the first time, we went days without speaking to one another, and the friction between the two of us was evident to anyone who happened to be in our company.

Yet despite the fissure that was between us, when it came to work, Susan was always there for me and I did my best to be there for her. Though, again, in hindsight, I could have done much more to cheer her up and encourage her.

Susan was still the first reader on every book I wrote, tweaking each chapter, asking questions about plot points and questioning why I was going in one direction with the story instead of another. She didn't read the scripts I wrote but always asked about them, tracking their development and eagerly watching the few that made their way to the screen. She was especially happy with my work on the NBC series *Law & Order*, since she was, much more than I had been prior to working there, a regular viewer of the show.

In that sense, we were a team and we knew that no disagreement, no hard feelings over any argument we may have had, would ever stand in the way of our working together. She was the best editor I ever worked with and was, by far, the best friend I would ever have. It was that friendship and mutual respect that allowed us to stay afloat despite the leaks in our marital boat.

THEN, ON THE Thursday before Presidents' Day weekend in February 2012, all of our silly arguments and disagreements were ground to dust.

I was in a gym in Sag Harbor, halfway through a workout, when my cell phone rang. My initial instinct was to dismiss the call. Susan was working with contractors and renovators who were in the middle of remodeling the Chelsea apartment, and the last thing I wanted to talk about was what would be the best color for the kitchen backsplash. To get away from the work, which was expected to take more than three months to complete, I had rented a house in the Hamptons to finish a book. Susan had sublet a small East Side apartment to be close to her newest job, and we would get together on the weekends.

I took the call and stepped out of the gym, drenched in sweat, standing in twenty-degree weather. Nick's voice sounded somber and sad. "Hi, Dad," he said. "I'm going to put Mom on the phone. She has something to tell you. Something serious."

I waited while Nick passed the phone to Susan. "I'm sorry to have to tell you like this," she said. "I wanted to tell you when I came out later this weekend."

"Tell me what?" I asked.

"The doctors want me to have surgery tomorrow morning," Susan said, her voice calm, betraying no hint of the bombshell that was to come. "That's why I have to tell you now, over the phone."

I began to shiver, partly from the cold and partly from the ugly feeling in the center of my chest and the middle of my stomach.

"Why do you need surgery?" I managed to ask, my teeth clenched, my face red from the sweat and the cold and the fear.

"I have stage-four lung cancer," Susan said. She waited a few moments, giving time for that horrible sentence to sink in. "There's a cloud around my lungs that the doctors want to remove so they can get a better sense of the damage."

"When did you find this out?" I asked, not bothering to mask my anger. "Why did you wait to tell me?"

"I found out earlier in the week, and I wanted to tell you while I was sitting across from you," Susan said. "I wasn't trying to hide it. I was just looking for the best way to let you know."

"How the hell did they only find it at stage four?" I said. "What happened to the other stages? You had no symptoms, right?"

"We'll talk about all that when I see you," Susan said. "And we'll know more once I have this surgery tomorrow. For now, we just have to wait."

"Where's the surgery?"

"Weill Cornell," Susan said. "But that's just for this surgery. I'm moving to Sloan Kettering to have them deal with the cancer. There's a doctor who has been recommended to me there, Gregory Riely. He's the best lung-cancer doctor they have, and he's the only chance I have to beat this disease."

"You'll beat it," I said, trying to sound somewhat upbeat. "If anyone can, you will. Look at how many other tumors you've beaten back in your life."

"Not this one," Susan said. "This one is a death sentence. I won't walk away from this one."

IT TOOK SIX weeks for Susan to recover from what had been described to me as minor surgery, removing the cloud surrounding her lungs, allowing Dr. Riely to decide on the best course of her treatment. Riely was indeed the best one to battle a disease that knew no surrender. He encouraged Susan not to lose hope, pointing out that every case was different and a quick ending was not the inevitable outcome. He and his team came up with a chemotherapy cocktail that allowed Susan to go on with her life with minimal impact. She swallowed dozens of pills a day and ate two pot-infused brownies a night. She continued her daily workouts and took her daily vitamins. She never missed a day of work, doing her job as a senior editor at *More* magazine and, during her lunch hour, walking over to a nearby Sloan Kettering chemo center for her three-days-a-week treatments.

Midway through 2012, Susan's treatments were going so well that Dr. Riely thought it would be okay for her to travel. Initially, we kept it simple. We went to Rockport, Maine, for a week to spend time at the Samoset Resort, where we owned a one-bedroom time-share. Susan had a healthy appetite, and we both drank more than our fair share of wine. It was a relaxing time, and for a short while we were allowed to push the word "cancer" into a dark corner.

But still, death's shadow lurked over our shoulders.

Susan and I were enjoying a long, slow walk in downtown Camden, Maine, in August of that year. The small fishing town had been one of our favorite places since our first visit there in the late 1980s. We walked past a small cemetery and stopped to gaze at the dates on the headstones, some of which went as far back as the 1700s.

"I need you to do me a favor," Susan said. "And I won't take no for an answer."

"I'm not going to ever say no," I said. "No matter what you ask me."

"It's about the book you're working on," Susan said.

I froze for a moment. It was no secret to either Susan, my editor, my agent, or my publisher that I was having trouble focusing on the novel. "What about it?" I asked.

"I would like you to finish it," Susan said. "It's a great idea, and I would like you to finish it so I can read it before I die."

"I'll finish it," I said. "But I don't want to hear anything about you dying. Look at how well you're doing. There are even moments when I forget you have cancer. You go to the gym and to work every day, you're eating and drinking, and you look great. You go to the theater with your friends. It's almost like it used to be. Maybe Dr. Riely found the perfect cocktail that will keep you alive."

"You're right about all that," Susan said. "But it can change in a day. That's what I have to live with, and I can handle that. Now, if you really want to help me, then as soon as we get back home, shut yourself in your office and finish this book."

"I will," I said. "It won't take long. I just need to get out of this corner I've put myself in with the plot. Once I figure that out, the story should move along on its own steam."

"Well, instead of talking about cancer, let's talk about your plot," Susan said. "That's a problem that can be solved."

I looked at her and smiled. "I would like that," I said. "I would like that very much."

"My editorial help doesn't come cheap," Susan said, also smiling. "Buy me an ice cream cone and then we'll talk."

And talk we did, sitting on a bench in a side street of Camden, Maine, breaking apart a problem with plot and characters. It was something we had done together so many times over so many years. And the very thought that there would come a day in the not-so-distant future that I wouldn't be able to sit with her and talk about a book I was writing, or one she was reading, or a movie or play or television series either one of us was watching, was heartbreaking.

Through the decades, lean years and flush, Susan was the creative center that held me together. At that very moment, in that sweet little town, I knew our years as a team were coming to an end. She was right: This cancer would end her life so much earlier than she deserved. And I had no idea if I would be able to survive her loss or even if I wanted to.

2013

WE TRAVELED AS often as Dr. Riely allowed and Susan was willing. Within a year, we went to Paris for a week, Rome for three weeks, the Hamptons for several long weekends, a return trip to Maine. The trips drew us closer, reminding both of us what we meant to each other and making me question the foolishness of the arguments that we did have.

When you are with someone you love and death is hanging over you, you pause and reflect on what you've both been through. I truly regretted every fight I ever had with Susan, questioning why any one of them was a cause for disagreement. Those were days and hours that could have been spent holding each other close. It is a sad weight to carry, and I do so every day.

I did go back and, with Susan's always capable editorial suggestions, finish the book I was writing. I handed her the completed third draft that I'd worked on with my then editor, Mark Tavani, and left her alone in the bedroom to read it.

A few hours later she came into the living room, where I was sitting, the manuscript clutched to her chest, walking slower now than she had in previous months. She had a smile on her face, and tears were forming in the corners of her eyes. "It's wonderful," she said. "One of your best in a long time. I'm glad I got to read it."

"No corrections?" I asked her. "Nothing you want me to change?"

"Not a thing," she said. "You and Mark did a great job. You should both be proud of the work."

"We should take a trip," I said. "I got an assignment from Bellows at the *Traveler*. That is, if you're up to going back to Italy."

"Where to this time?" Susan asked.

"Lake Como," I said. "Seems like the perfect place for a trip."

Susan nodded. "It is a perfect place," she said. "Let's do it soon. Just in case."

I nodded and watched my wife turn and head slowly back to the bedroom, the manuscript still clutched to her chest.

LAKE COMO WOULD prove to be our final trip together. It was a happy and sad week for us both, a special time in a setting that seemed magical. We stayed at the Villa d'Este and walked the grounds each day, holding hands and talking about our past and what the future held. It was on this trip, across those seven memorable days, where we both faced her imminent death head-on.

I had never felt closer to her than during that one-week period. She talked about our kids, what she hoped for them, how much she would miss them. We laughed as we recalled the early years, living together in secret, always on the verge of getting caught, taking it one moment at a time and enjoying every single second.

We talked about the various trips and adventures we shared with our kids and how much fun we all had traveling together. "Remember the time Nick crashed the golf cart into those two old women during that sunset tour we took at the Samoset?" I asked.

"No," Susan said, laughing. "I remember the time *you* let him drive the golf cart and he crashed into those poor old women."

"He was jealous because, two carts ahead, he saw you letting Kate drive," I said.

"She was ten," Susan said, "and Nick was only six."

"It caused a four-golf-cart pileup," I said. "Since that happened, he's never wanted to be anywhere near the state of Maine."

"And remember during our first time in Ischia, when Nick had that terrible headache?" Susan asked.

"You were going to give him some liquid Tylenol," I said. "Until my Aunt Anna filled a glass halfway up with water and then poured in a bunch of salt."

"I wondered what the hell she was doing," Susan said. "And I knew whatever it was would never work."

"She put a thick dish towel over the glass and then plopped it upside down on the top of Nick's head," I said. "I saw the look in your eye. You thought we were all crazy."

"I did," Susan said. "Until about ten minutes later, when the water in the glass started to boil. His headache went away a few seconds after that."

"He got too much sun," I said. "And the boiling water pulled the excess heat off his head. I bet they didn't work any magic like that back in the Mayo Clinic, where you were born."

"No, they didn't," Susan said. "But I tried it myself once when Kate was out by the pool for too long. Followed your aunt's method down to the right amount of salt."

"Did it work?"

"Doesn't it always?" Susan said.

We talked about everything that week, saving the one subject that most needed to be discussed until the last day. We were on a boat, one that took us from one lake town to the next. Along the scenic route, we passed the villas owned by George Clooney, Versace, Richard Branson, and some Italian royalty whose names didn't register. We took no photos, just sat and enjoyed the quiet of the water and the beauty of our surroundings.

"I know they're both out of college and on their own," Susan said. "But you still need to be there for them. There'll come a time when they'll need you, for advice, guidance, or just to talk. When that time comes, you need to be there."

"I will," I said.

"And they'll be there for you. They're terrific kids. We got that part right."

"You more than me," I said. "You put in a lot more time than I did."

"You did more than your share," Susan said. "You took almost half a year off to take care of Kate when she was about four and you freelanced at night."

"And how well did that turn out?" I asked, smiling at the memory.

"Other than letting her watch *Jaws* when she was barely five, you did better than okay," Susan said. "To this day, she's afraid of going into ocean water because of sharks."

"As much your fault as it is mine," I said.

"How is it my fault?"

"You came home from work that night and there were still about ten minutes to go in the movie," I said. "You were so stunned we were watching it that you ran over to the VCR machine and turned it off."

"So?"

"So she never got to see the end of the movie," I said. "Never got to see the shark get killed. You left her with the idea that he lived. That's why she's afraid of the ocean."

"The two of you should keep with your Christmas movie tradition," Susan said. "Odd as your choices are."

"There's no beating watching *Angels with Dirty Faces* and *Abbott and Costello Meet Frankenstein,*" I said. "Should be a tradition in every home."

"You could never rope Nick in, though," Susan said. "No matter how hard you both tried."

"He prefers *Die Hard*," I said. "Where did I go wrong?"

"I suppose it's too late to compromise on *It's a Wonderful Life?*" Susan said.

"That ship, just like the one we're on, has sailed," I said, reaching for and holding her hand.

"We still never found one great movie we both could agree on," Susan said. "After all these years."

"Yes, we did," I said. "Last summer up in Maine, remember? We sat through it twice, both times laughing our asses off."

Susan nodded and smiled. *"Ted,"* she said. "You're right. That one movie we both loved. Thank God for Seth MacFarlane and Mark Wahlberg."

That night we had dinner at a hilltop restaurant called Il Gatto Nero. As we looked down, Lake Como glowed under the moonlight and seemed to curve off into the distance forever. "Take some time for yourself after all this is over," Susan said. "But then you need to get back to work."

"I don't want to talk about this now," I said.

"This is *the* time to talk about it," Susan said. "I don't have much time left."

"Dr. Riely tell you that?"

"He doesn't need to," she said. "I know my body, and I can feel I'm running short of time. So, like it or not, you need to listen to what I have to say."

"I'll keep working," I said. "As no one knows better than you, I don't know how to do anything else. Plus, writing is the only time I can put aside the things in my life I did wrong and not think about the people I loved who are no longer here. I've always been able to do that. I just don't know if I'll be able to do it without you around."

* * *

THAT FALL, SUSAN'S decline began.

All of November and the early parts of December were spent in and out of Sloan Kettering. She underwent two surgeries to help ease her pain. Neither was truly effective. She lost weight, wasn't eating, and needed full-time nursing care. Kate and Nick stepped up and I watched as they hovered over their mother, breaking down the pills she needed to take, keeping the visiting nurses up to date on what she ate and how long she slept. They made her laugh when she was at her lowest and cried when she was out of their sight. They made sure that one or the other was always by her side.

Susan loved Christmas and decorating the tree with family ornaments. She did this with our children each year during our long marriage, and it was a tradition the three enjoyed more than any other. As her condition continued to deteriorate, an oxygen tank now always by her side, Susan asked if we could decorate the tree earlier than usual and also if we could invite some of her friends to help.

Kate made the arrangements and planned it for the first Saturday in December. More than twenty of Susan's closest friends came that afternoon. There was wine and champagne. Sandwich and salad platters were spread throughout the apartment. Susan sat in a chair closest to a window, a wide smile on her face as she watched her friends take turns placing her cherished ornaments on the huge tree we had purchased.

I sat next to her and she smiled. "It looks great, doesn't it?" she said. "And it will look even better when the lights are turned on."

I could only nod. I didn't need doctors to tell me this would be my wife's last Christmas, her final time spent in the company of people she had known for decades. "You want some wine?" I managed to ask.

"Some water, maybe," she said in a soft voice. "Or ice chips might be better."

I went to the kitchen and filled a cup with ice chips. I looked across the room at Susan and then at Kate, and we both exchanged a sad smile. I walked the ice chips back to Susan and sat down by her side again.

"Do something nice with them on Christmas," she said. "It's their favorite holiday."

"Sure," I said. "Where do you want to go?"

"Not me," Susan said. "Just you and them."

I swallowed hard. "Where should I take them?" I asked. "You're the one who always plans these things. You know how much I suck at that."

"Well, you're going to have to get better at it," Susan said. "You've seen me do it enough times to have learned a few things. Kate will help. Nick, too."

"Okay," I said.

"Be there for each other," she said. "It's important to me, and it will be important for the three of you. The five of you, if you want to count Gus and Willow. Can't forget the dogs."

"Never," I said.

"Let that be your gift to me," she said. "Your last gift. Always be there for them and for each other. And don't forget: Keep writing those stories. I don't want to be the excuse for you no longer telling them."

"I always told you the stories before I wrote them," I said.

"Now tell the stories to them," she said. "They'll listen, same as I did. And they'll tell you if you're on the right track or not. Will you do that for me?"

I nodded.

"I can't think of a better gift," Susan said.

"I can't, either," I said.

I held her thin, frail hand in mine, and we spent the rest of the time watching her friends finish decorating the last Christmas tree my wife would ever see.

SUSAN DIED ON Christmas Eve 2013.

As I write this, more than seven years have passed since her death. In that time, our daughter, Kate, married a wonderful man she loves dearly and on December 4, 2019, gave birth to their first child, Oliver Lorenzo Wood. It would have been magical for Susan to be here to witness that moment.

Nick works hard and has many close friends and is always there in a time of need. Both my kids are. They make sure I never get too down, and we see each other as often as possible. No father could ask for better children, and I have only my wife to thank for that. Each time I see them, I hear her voice and I see her smile and I feel her love through them.

I did take time off from writing after Susan's death. Probably more than I should. In 2017, I started to write books again, and this will be the third I've completed since she lost her bout to lung cancer.

I went at the books with a newfound drive and determination. I felt refueled and energized. I devoted my time to work on the stories Susan so much liked to hear me talk about. And I never feel alone when I'm writing them. She is there with me.

An editor on my shoulder.

She is never far removed from my thoughts, and I feel her presence daily. I miss my wife a great deal.

But I miss my good friend even more.

And I always will.

EPILOGUE

❧

Summer 2019

TWO SUMMERS AGO, while visiting Ischia, I took my two grown children—Kate and Nick—to the cemetery to see Nonna Maria and Nonno Gabriel. Going to Ischia has become a yearly tradition for me and my children, especially in the years since their mother and my wife died.

It was their first time visiting the cemetery. It's a well-maintained and peaceful place, drenched in sunlight, with full views of the bay in the distance. We stood before the marble wall and looked up at the names of my grandparents etched across the stone. Their dates of birth and death were also chiseled in, and a photo of each one rested alongside their name.

"I didn't think it would be like this," Kate said, looking around the cemetery. "It's just so beautiful."

Nick studied Nonna's picture. "I never knew what she looked like," he said. "You talk about her so much, but I never saw any pictures of her. Until now."

"There weren't many cameras around," I said. "And Nonna wasn't eager to have her photo taken."

"It's nice that they're both next to each other," Kate said.

I nodded and stepped closer to the wall. I reached up a hand and ran my fingers across the base of the marble. I stared up at Nonna's photo and smiled, tears forming at the corners of my eyes.

"Thank you, Nonna," I whispered. "Thank you so much."

I pressed my fingers to my lips and then back onto the marble. One kiss each for my Nonna and for Nonno.

I then turned, my children on each side of me, and we slowly walked out of the cemetery.

I turned to look back at them and was happy to see that my grandparents were where they belonged.

Forever together.

ACKNOWLEDGMENTS

WRITING ABOUT MY Nonna, my mother, and my wife would not have been possible without the extraordinary group of women in my life. To each of them I owe a debt of gratitude and a piece of my heart.

Suzanne Gluck fell in love with the idea of this book as soon as she heard it and then convinced me to write an outline and then followed it through every step of the way.

To my great crew at Ballantine and Random House—from Gina Centrello, who has never stopped believing in me, to Kara Welsh and Jennifer Hershey, who never fail to cheer me on and always have my back. And to my great editor, Anne Speyer, who made each and every page of this book better with her skill and passion. They have all earned their place of honor among the Three Dreamers.

And to the women whose friendship and love I would be lost without—first among them the amazing Mary Ellen Keating, who fought a tough and valiant fight against a brutal disease and didn't quit until she won the battle. She has the kindest heart of anyone I know. It is an honor to have her by my side. To Leah Rozen, Dorothy Bertucci, Carol Berry, Angela Rumore, Ida Cerbone, Sandi Mendelsohn, Adriana Trigiani, Andrea Blatt, and Joyce and Charmain—thank you for your friendship and kindness.

I'm a lucky man to have all these great women on my side. And I'm thankful for it each and every day.

LORENZO CARCATERRA is the #1 *New York Times* bestselling author of *A Safe Place, Sleepers, Apaches, Gangster, Street Boys, Paradise City, Chasers, Midnight Angels, The Wolf, Tin Badges, Payback, Three Dreamers,* and *Nonna Maria and the Case of the Missing Bride.* He is a former writer/producer for *Law & Order* and has written for *National Geographic Traveler, The New York Times Magazine,* and *Maxim.* He lives in New York City.

lorenzocarcaterra.com